THE ROAD TO PURPOSE

THE ROAD TO PURPOSE

The Roadmap for
Overcoming Life's Major Transitions

GREG A. PESTINGER

IGNITE
PRESS
Fresno, CA

Published in the United States by Ignite Press.
ignitepress.us

ISBN: 978-1-950710-76-8 (Amazon Print)
ISBN: 978-1-950710-77-5 (IngramSpark) PAPERBACK
ISBN: 978-1-950710-78-2 (IngramSpark) HARDCOVER
ISBN: 978-1-950710-79-9 (Smashwords)

For bulk purchase and for booking, contact:

Greg A. Pestinger
www.p3peakperformance.com

Library of Congress Control Number: 2020916683

Edited by Samantha Maxwell
Interior design by Evolve Layout Services

This book is dedicated to all who have found the courage to face life's most difficult transitions, to learn and grow from their experiences, and to realize a life of meaning and purpose in service to others.

Aspire to Inspire
GREATNESS!

Acknowledgements

It has been said that a life well lived takes a village. For me, that has been a village of family, friends, fraternity brothers, mentors, clients, coaches, and an incredible team of passionate and caring people at P3 Peak Performance. A team of people who have helped me become a better version of myself, often through struggle, without judgement, but always with my best interest in mind. They are too many to list in this space, yet I would like to call attention to a few significant names that made *The Road to Purpose* possible.

For my wife, Donna Pestinger, my biggest cheerleader. She is by my side while climbing my highest mountains or clawing my way back from the depths of hell. She shows me through good and not so good that she is always there. That in a world that can be less than civil, goodness always reigns supreme. She is my grace on earth.

To my mother and father, Kathleen and Gene Pestinger, who taught me that anything is possible if you are willing to work for it and that with success comes a responsibility to your community and support for others who need your help. For never accepting anything less than my best, for loving me even in times when I wasn't very likable. For the freedom to pursue my own dreams and the accountability to make those dreams come true.

To my brothers in Sigma Phi Epsilon fraternity who taught me that through our cardinal principles of virtue, diligence, and brotherly love, that life has meaning and purpose. Especially for those exceptional brothers trying to find their own way in the world, who shared their struggles with mental health, allowed themselves to be vulnerable, and used that struggle to help others. They are true heroes, an inspiration, and they are setting the stage for an incredible future ahead of us. A special few who participated in my performance coaching program have impacted me in amazing ways and have gone on to do great things in their lives. A special thank you to Ben Hutto, Brad Hoffman, Jake Bension, Jonathan Salmen, Ryan Ware, Salvador Zaragoza, David O'Coffey, Francisco Rios, and Ian Pitt for trusting me with your lives and teaching me about my own through our time together, time that was the inspiration for the company we have today. And for those who welcomed me back when I had lost my way: Brian Warren, Brian Delaney, Davis Orr, Kevin Knudson, Garry Kief, Jay Hurt, Austin McCraw, Kelly Williams, Brad Nahrstadt, and the men on the quest. I would not be half the man I am today if not for your time in my life. I have very big shoes to fill and am eternally grateful.

My mentors over the years. I have been blessed with the best of the best, some younger and some older, who have cared enough to share themselves with me even when I was pushing them away. Their teachings formed the man I have become, a go-to source of wisdom that I use to this day to teach others. Guardian angels in both my professional and personal life including Grandma Dowd, Dean Campbell, Margie Walsh, Tom Kreft, Ann Stickler, Steve Thompson, George Demaree, Jeri Swinton, my coaches and business partners, and especially, my clients. I often leave our time together inspired to do more. It is said that "you learn most from teaching others..." Nothing could be truer when I am with you. Since the road to purpose, two of my early mentors, Denis Shumate and Ron Becker, have passed on. They had a profound impact on me growing up and continued to show interest in me well into adulthood. They will be greatly missed, but in some way, I hope that they live on in me through the lessons I learned and the responsibility I feel to pass that on to the young men I mentor.

I often wonder if I am "uncoachable." As a coach myself, I know how difficult it can be to work with someone like me. I also know the life-changing work a great coach can provide. It took a small army of coaches to push this uncoachable person forward. They never gave up and never accepted anything other than my best. To Margaret Maclay, my business coach, who provided the business foundation to give me the means and the mindset to complete this project. She helped me get out of my head during the difficult startup year and focus my energy on intention to build my business. To Jeff Nally and Cara Silletto, world class business owners, executive coach, employee retention expert and NSA professional speakers who are helping me help others by bringing this book to life through speaking engagements. To my Tony Robbins Performance Coach, Keith Waggoner, a man whose purpose is to help other men, men like me, find the fulfillment of a balanced life and to live the life of meaning and purpose entrusted to us by the master of the universe. To Cathy Fyock, my book coach. She kept me going even when the words weren't there, the stories were not connecting, and the sometimes-dark days I experienced when I simply did not want to write.

To my editorial board who spent tireless hours reading through many early drafts, fighting my sometimes "creative" use of the English language in this book to make sure that it would provide value to my readers by connecting on a deeply personal level with all of you. Thank you, Jake Bension, Ryan Ware, Donna Pestinger, Cathy Fyock, Kathleen Pestinger, and Ignite Press for the sacrifice of your time to care about this project as much as I did and to care about me enough to see me through. Without your support, this book would not have ever made it to print.

To all those who hosted me along the road to purpose. This book is about you and the life-changing lessons I learned simply by spending time with you along the way. This book is for you, Jeff, Kim and Cooper Tennant, Ron and Debbie Heinrich, Kelli and Mike Spaulding, Julie Jackson, Riley Norton, Jeff and Lori Pestinger, Maureen Dowd, Nick Schlyer, Shannon and Shelly Batman, Ray Norman, Todd Kirsch, Timmy, Laura, Tommy and Doris Pestinger, Russ Anspaugh, Tom Jadlow, Ken Corsini, Drew Wojcik, Rob and Penny Schlyer, Ginny Tennant, and all the others who took time out of their days, last minute, to join me for dinner or a cold beer along the way. For the warm beds, the cold beers, the home-cooked meals, and especially for sharing your families with me. I am forever grateful.

Now it's my turn to help others navigate their own roads of life. To continue the legacy of those who got me to where I am today by helping others find their own path. To live a life of meaning and purpose and to extend the meaning and purpose of those who came before.

Finally, I am grateful to the master of the universe who blesses us all with a unique meaning and purpose the day we are born, the challenge to find out exactly what that is and the talent to bring it to life with others along the road to purpose.

Table of Contents

THE COURAGE TO BE YOURSELF

RESOLVE TO LOVE YOURSELF

A Letter to My Reader

"The only impossible journey is
the one you don't begin."

—Tony Robbins

Why Are We So Empty Inside?

In all of human history, there has never been a better time to be alive. Advancements in science and technology have put at our very fingertips all that we can imagine, every opportunity that we could ever hope for. People today are more educated, more passionate, and wealthier than they have ever been in all other decades combined. Yet we are empty inside. It seems that the harder we try to achieve nirvana, the further we fall behind. Suicide rates are up in almost all categories; stress, anxiety, and depression are at an all-time high, and relief is nowhere in sight.

I was one of those guys who had achieved many of my dreams, one of those guys who had spent a lifetime collecting things, promotions, and other symbols that, in some way, said to others that I had made it. The reality was that I didn't like myself much—that I was suffering from ongoing mental health struggles and covering them up by staying busy. I made it a point to shun vulnerability of any kind to prove I was strong. All the while, I felt empty inside. I was headed down an unsustainable path. In short, while I was successful, I wasn't fulfilled by the success I had achieved.

Then it happened. Without warning, my company sold a group of brands, and my job was eliminated. I was 50 years old, a 30-year veteran of corporate life, highly compensated, and out of work. Worse yet, I had twice passed on an offer to run my own family business and had instead spent those 30 years defining who I was by my work, by what I did. I was not only out of work; I was now out of what I thought at the time to be meaning and purpose. I was devastated, I questioned life itself, and my perfect world spiraled down a black hole. My life as I had known it was over.

Why I Chose to Write This Book

Let me be clear: I never thought I would be where I am today. I never thought I would be writing a book, never had a goal to write a book; I would not put writing of any kind in the top 100 things that I enjoy doing.

So why did I write this book? Simply put, I wanted to help people whose lives, lives full of certainty, suddenly went off the rails because of no fault of their own. People who worked hard all their lives who were suddenly forced down a path they never intended, one that was uncertain, full of fear and self-doubt — one that forced them to question who they were as a person and whether or not their entire lives had been for naught.

I was one of those people with a spotless, successful, 30-year career with some of America's top companies and was faced with the fact that those companies would decide that the business I managed was no longer critical. After spotless reviews, record results, and and connections with an incredible network of people, my job ended without notice upon the sale of the business to a competitor. Even though the outcome had everything to do with a change in direction for the company and nothing to do with me, I blamed myself, questioned my very existence, and filled my every thought with paralyzing self-doubt, anger, and very low self-esteem. Here I was after 30 years of successful work, over 50 and out of work, and with nothing to show for it except an overwhelming feeling of worthlessness, fear, rejection, and the very dark pits of depression.

As many experiencing similar circumstances, I would suspect others may be doing the same, believing that the misfortune that came upon them was about them. That we had done something wrong or that we were flawed in some way. I think that's a normal reaction, but here is what I learned: It's not about you at all. Companies, universities, and organizations all do things for their reasons; it's part of the very fabric of public companies whose sole purpose it is to make money for their shareholders first. So, the first thing we must do is get over the notion that something is wrong with us. If you want to blame yourself for something, the fact is that all you can say is that you were in the wrong place at the wrong time. I know you're hurting, and it's hard to see that now, but you will, and when you do, it will set you free.

I wrote this book because what followed this period were some of the most incredible, rewarding, and thought-provoking events of my entire life, a life that would have never happened had it not been for the series of seemingly random and meaningless situations that ended up forcing me to take a different and painful look at my life. A life that required me to blaze a new path, one that set the stage for the rest of my time on earth. A way that I was always intended to take. A path that would define who I am and why it mattered to those I would soon help. I wrote this book because what I found was that as I committed to helping others, I was in a way helping myself find my meaning and purpose. I wrote this book because I too want to see you push through your pain to a world that, like mine, has been nothing short of grace.

I hope that by sharing my troubled journey, I can change all that for the reader. That in some way, I can help you see that the beauty that lies on the other side of uncertainty is worth the wait, that what seems like random circumstances can become "intention" for you to work your own way through the pain and in turn realize the growth it produces.

Who This Book Is For

This book is for anyone facing the uncertainty that often comes with a significant life transition. This book is for students who are approaching their final year in school before they venture out into the "real world" with no idea of what they want to do. This book is for their parents, guardians, mentors, coaches, and teachers who are trying to help them navigate the changes that are ahead. This book is also for the employee who is approaching their final decade of work and facing the uncertain risk that comes with late-life job layoffs and corporate reorganizations. This book is for the business owner who, after decades of building a company, is now faced with the psychological difficulty of retiring or walking away.

This book is for anyone who is leaving what they have always known to be true for something unknown and facing the fear and anxiety that comes with it. Transition is difficult and often comes with fear, anger, and questions of self-worth that can lead to a feeling of emptiness. What seems at the time to be a life "happening to you" is actually "happening for you," an experience where the loss of control and the random misfortune will soon grow into the unimaginable life of transformation that I share with you in the pages that follow. Like so many times in life, when a significant transition occurs, it impacts those of us who have lived a determined and intentional life more than others. Like all hard-working, loyal high-achievers that I would meet along the journey, the perfect life that they had worked so hard for would prove to be fleeting.

What I also found was that the uncertainty felt by young people figuring out what they want to do and those in the final decade of work, now facing what they wanted to do next, was not all that different. The emotion experienced was precisely the same. For both generations, the transition is genuine and very scary and can lead to traumatic and devastating events, including addiction, depression, anxiety, and at a growing and alarming rate, the extreme, suicide.

No one chooses this life, the life I had four years ago, nor would I wish it on anyone. What came from my own experience, the people I met, and their stories of uncertainty have inspired me to share these stories and the courage they mustered to face the challenges that laid ahead. What I do know is that what I experienced was not in any way unique to me. What I found was that friends and coworkers were experiencing similar difficulties.

The Road to Purpose tells the story of a spontaneous road trip taken out of anger and desperation after experiencing my own forced transition and the lessons I learned along the way. The journey spanned over two months and followed a random and spontaneous path through 32 states by car, often spending the night with friends, cousins, fraternity brothers, in the occasional cheap hotel, or sleeping in my car along the route.

The pages that follow begin with the overwhelming circumstances that resulted in my career ending. It then progresses through the emotional rollercoaster that followed as I transformed through those experiences to the beautiful life I have today. These lessons are brought to life through stories that hit me square between the eyes through the people I met. Stories that forced me to shut up, give up the need to be in control, and listen, to understand what they had to say. Other times, those lessons came to me in discussions with myself that happened during long days all alone in a car with no one to talk to but myself. Lessons learned, and the opportunity to use those lessons in service to others, have become my purpose and have resulted in a life of happiness, prosperity, and meaning.

Ride along with me as I revisit the people and places that made up the road to purpose. Each chapter will follow the same approach: 1. the story that supplied the opportunity for that growth, 2. a reference to the social media journal entry that I posted each day to bring to life my thinking at the moment, and 3. the lesson learned. You will notice that when I refer to the journal entry, I will make a statement like "Returning to the road to purpose" followed by the post. You can skip this part if you like. It doesn't interrupt the content of the book; it merely adds a little flavor to the passage. At the end of each chapter, I will leave you with signposts or tips to apply in your life today.

The stories then and the impact they have had on my life since have been nothing short of transformational. The lessons I learned along the way have worked for me in the time since I made my journey of self-discovery, and I hope in some way that they will have the same impact on you. I hope that just maybe *The Road to Purpose* provides you with a thought or two that helps guide you through the fear and uncertainty that is part of your transition and enables you to push beyond that fear to realize the incredible life that lies ahead.

Whether you are a young adult moving from school to your first career, a business owner getting ready to exit your business, or a seasoned executive figuring out what to do next, you will see yourself in the stories that follow. You will experience the pain, the grace, and the learning from one man's journey that resulted in living a life of meaning and purpose, a life full of wealth, happiness, and intention in service to others.

I believe that life has meaning and purpose. I believe that every one of us can realize our greatest dreams and reach our full potential. I hope that this book helps you navigate your journey. Utilize the simple tools, techniques, and strategies outlined in the pages ahead to help you reach your full potential so that you, too, can live a life of meaning and purpose.

Believe, "Aspire to Inspire Greatness"

Greg A. Pestinger
Certified Performance Coach, Mentor, and Trainer
CEO and Founder, Pestinger Peak Performance Inc.
President, FocalPoint Coaching and Training Excellence of Kentucky

SECTION 1

THE CHALLENGE TO
KNOW YOURSELF

"Knowing yourself is the beginning of all wisdom."

—Aristotle

Chapter 1

Bliss and Heartbreak

*"I am not what has happened to me;
I am what I choose to become."*

—Carl Jung

The Day That Changed Everything

At 8:45 a.m. on an early morning in January, it was a typical day for me at my company. I thought to myself, "What a great place to work. I'm so fortunate to work here and grateful for my team, my friends, and the opportunity to do the work I love every day." I pinched myself as I thought about the global iconic brands I was working on and cherished the envy my friends and family bestowed upon me for the prestige that came with working with the brands. There was something about this place that felt like being a part of something much bigger than myself, more like a family business and not what I expected from a $3 billion company.

My very first day just happened to be at the annual shareholders meeting. For this company, the day was jokingly called "the family reunion," given that the company was still controlled by the founding family, now in its sixth generation.

The annual shareholders meeting was followed by the vice president of my group presenting new marketing changes to a private meeting of the family. My boss, another coworker, and I were stoically seated at the front of the room, facing the crowd as our leader presented the changes to an iconic package. I had just returned to Louisville for this opportunity after being gone for a long time with several other leading companies, and this was my first day back. There on the front row were a lady and gentleman who continued to stare at me as if they knew me—and believe me, I knew them.

After the meeting, they approached me and called me by name. The woman had remembered me from a nonprofit project that I had worked on under her leadership. Their name was on the building, and their values permeated the company where I worked. She had remembered me, just an average person volunteering on a project that I had been involved with over ten years ago. Incredible people, kind, intelligent, engaged. And at that moment, I knew I was where I was supposed to be.

My career had always been my social currency: It challenged me, it made me better. My work had become, in all senses of the word, me. The very way I defined myself, the source of my pleasure, my self-esteem, and my motivation. I was living my dream and grateful for the life it provided me.

That January morning felt especially useful for me. I was working with an incredible team of people, and the Vice President who I worked for had just given me one of the best performance reviews that I had ever experienced. Over the years, we had gone through a lot together and had created world-class marketing that moved the needle on aging but iconic brands. She had become a friend and a mentor and had always been there for my team and me. I knew that our work was essential to her, and she often showed it by encouraging my young team and their intrapreneurial approach to the traditional brands. She knew her stuff and was an incredible marketer, a great motivator of people, and she was someone willing to do whatever it took to get the job done.

Toward the end of my review, nervous with what I wanted to share about some organizational thoughts, I asked, "What if we move some people around on my team to better align talent with the work? We could put..."

Her head dropped, silence followed, and before I could finish, she just said, "I can't," and got up to leave for a meeting. That was unlike her. It registered and hurt a little, but I shook it off to be just the typical "crazy busy" of the New Year. I thought nothing of it, and with a smile and a hop in my step, I left her office to get back to my team.

As my team began to show up that morning, I could see them shaking off the brisk winter morning and getting ready to get going on the new year. My team was nothing short of amazing, relatively young, and all energetic marketers with a passion for making an impact on the company and the communities where we did business. They would create new growth with limited resources and a lot of creativity that would make a real difference for their brands, their customers, and for the company. It was precisely that, a great team doing great work, that made coming to work so rewarding.

The smell of freshly brewed coffee from the break room and the sound of a copy machine running off presentation decks began to fill the air. Just in from the cold, damp January outside, warm and cozy inside, people were holding their coffee cups close as they checked in before sitting down to work. Over the weekend, a calendar invite had come through for a meeting that was scheduled for 8:45. As the time approached, we began the short walk to the conference room. When we arrived, it dawned on us that the only people in the room were our team, less my boss. Had something happened with her?

Small talk just above a whisper had begun, questioning the reason for the impromptu meeting. Soon after, the Chief Marketing Officer and Chief People Officer walked in. The room became quiet as the Chief People Officer uttered the words that I will never forget, "We have sold our second-largest brand and will be announcing that sale to Wall Street at 9 a.m. All of you in this room are affected, and your HR professional will be sitting down with you to talk about options."

My mind began to race, *What did she say? No, I must have misunderstood it*. I asked a clarifying question, "What does that mean for the team?" The response in a monotone, robot-like way, "You have all been affected, and your HR manager will get with you." My heart stopped beating; I could feel anger rising in my body as if it were an elevator shooting to the top floor of a building. Disappointment, disdain, and worry began to flood every part of my being.

All around me became a blur as my mind told me to focus on my team. One member, in particular, had just been promoted less than two months prior, and she looked at me and began to cry. What happens next? "Your HR manager will get with you." The room became eerily silent. Soon the sound of sniffles and later total despair echoed the halls. "Bam," a door slammed shut as people made beelines to their offices. Some were angry, some crying, others with a distinct look of shock in their eyes. Several employees had been with the company for more than 20, some 30 years, and it was all gone based on the decision to sell off a brand. I did my best to comfort those close to me without much luck.

I'm sure they could see the fear in my eyes as the tears began to flow. For the first time, I didn't know what to do next. My work family was falling apart, and I could do nothing about it. It was one of the loneliest times in my life. I was so overwhelmed with the impact on my team that I had not fully realized the effect on me. It became clear that the greatest fear of my middle-age life had become a reality. I will never forget those words, "Your human resources professional will be meeting with each of you individually to work on the next steps. You are welcome to apply for open positions, but if not, your final day with the company will be March 6th."

I also felt stupid that I hadn't seen this coming. I thought about the many times when I would praise the company to others, I would often be warned just how ruthless it could be. I was angry and looking for something to blame, and the company was on top of that list. I think I knew deep inside that this is just what companies do, but in my sometimes overly optimistic mind, it wasn't what companies did to me. Worst of all was the letdown I felt from my boss: Yesterday, the best review of my life; today, job eliminated. As my mind raced for answers, I needed someone to blame, and that laid squarely in her lap. In my mind, she had deceived me, and that hurt more than any other part of it. As our brains often do when under severe stress, it made up reasons like, "She used me then threw me out like the garbage." I hated her and didn't trust her and all she stood for.

I would later learn that her job was on the line, and she would have suffered severe consequences if she shared what was to occur before the announcement. With time, the anger began to subside, and things did start to come back together. A few of the team members would go for the open positions in the company, and I got to write recommendation letters and talk with new hiring managers before I left on their behalf. It felt good to be supporting my teammates one last time. For me, after seeing the previous two companies I worked for both going through reorganizations and the impact it had on the people who worked there, I chose to try my luck in the outside world.

For my boss and I, it had been about two months since the announcement, and our friendship had started to heal. Our discussions were pleasant and focused on the future. We've shared many lunches over the years since, and I still cherish my time with her.

Resume's Out, No Callbacks

Well, the time had come for me to start thinking about what was next. I had decided that I was not going to stay, and as every comfortable corporate type does, I picked myself up and updated my resume. I was offered outplacement as part of my severance package and laughed at it, asking for the money instead. It was, of course, denied, so I dipped my toe in to see what this outplacement thing was all about.

I learned a few things that I didn't expect, like when you're over 50 that you have an entirely different approach to resume writing and the job market. Still bitter, I listened, but of course, knew better and did it my way. After all, in my entire 30-year corporate career, there was only one job I went for that I didn't get. Why would it be different now? I would find out later that it was going to be very different this time. I was over 50, highly compensated (their words, not mine), and for the most part, pigeonholed as a marketer. I was channeling my anger into getting my dream job with a top craft brewery, swearing off large companies forever. Neither became a reality. Every day and no reply became very real. I was not taking care of myself, not sleeping became the norm, and inside, my mind was driving me deeper and deeper into despair.

Then I was punched in the face with a completely new and extremely humiliating experience, one that to this day has changed how I look at people who are out of work. Part of that process was filing for unemployment for the first time. It was one of the most embarrassing, humiliating experiences that I had ever had. I ignored this at first, given my ego was stronger than the embarrassment of waiting in line to get a government handout. Later, at the advice of many I trusted, I did make the trip, and it was as horrible as I had pictured it to be.

The experience would push me to an even deeper level of despair, and each week with a new check came the reminder that I was worthless, that no one would hire me. Depression soon set in, and I lost all interest in things I had once enjoyed, like working out, learning new things, and hanging out with the people I loved. I quietly retreated from my friends and family, too embarrassed to face them. For me, a life without meaning was not worth the time of day, and I began to see myself as just taking up space.

It didn't help that I would have to report the jobs that I had provided applications for each week. I had to work, and even though applying for jobs was another reminder of my value, I immediately started reaching out to the business I knew best: beer. Beer was the answer, and craft brewing would be my target. I thought to myself, "This is a sure thing, who wouldn't hire a person with my vast experience and record of success?" I thought, "They need me."

Well, as it would go, I got next to zero callbacks. I thought to myself, "Their loss. That's why they are small anyway." My sarcasm quickly turned to anger, depression, and regret, and with the voices in my head confirming my worthlessness, I began to give up. You know those voices that fill our heads when a traumatic occurrence happens in our lives? I was saying, "You idiot, you will never get another job like the one you left. You're too old, you're overweight, you're too expensive. No one wants you." As the days passed and I was reminded each month of the unemployment request, I fell further and further down the rabbit hole. Ending it all had crossed my mind, and I knew that I had to do something, or it was not going to go well for me. I was giving up.

A Ride on the Emotional Rollercoaster

Wow, was the universe punching me in the face. Not only was my corporate life a mess over the ongoing humiliating experience of unemployment, now no one was calling me back for what should have been slam-dunk job applications. The voices in my head were working overtime: "Your life is over. You can't even get a beer job." Fear and anger began to pile on, then blame, excuses, and holding grudges. If the world was done with me, then I was done with the world. Depression now had a firm grasp around my neck, and it was starting to impact my relationships with the people I loved and cared for most. Facing my family, confident, hardworking, and successful people, was the hardest part. The very people who had been the example of overcoming the odds were now a reminder of my failure.

I found myself for the first time in my life without any options. So, what did I do? Well, I took all that anger, depression, and denial and decided to run away. I decided that I needed a change of pace to snap back into my old self, hopefully. That decision manifested itself in a random road trip across the United States. I would just wander for a few months across the country, seeing people, places, and things that I had neglected for so long while I was climbing what I thought was the ladder of success. For me, to do anything unplanned was out of character, way outside my comfort zone. Now I had nothing to lose, so I did just that. What at the time I thought to be giving up and running away from life turned out to be what I needed to do.

It's important to note for future reference that just before leaving, a couple of random and unexplained things happened. At the time, I thought nothing of it, but now I know that they were part of a master plan for the very trip I was about to take. The first was a webinar. Remember that outplacement company? Well, it had posted an invitation to a class called "From Corporate Life to Business Ownership." It barely registered at the time but stuck with me. I had been down this path before and had decided to walk away from a great opportunity running my own family business.

The second was a social media post that inspired me to get back involved in my fraternity as a volunteer mentor after 30 years away, chasing the proverbial dream of corporate domination. Not only did this come into my life at precisely the right time, but later on, I would find out a young brother had lost his battle with depression before I started my work with the chapter. That would light a spark deep inside my heart that would grow into a massive bonfire over the next few years, one that has become a primary driver in the life that I lead today, the vision to end the epidemic of suicide in young people.

My experience with this group has left me with awe and wonder. Young men at the very beginning of life, full of hope, courage, and compassion getting ready to take on the world—change it really—but they're empty inside. Full of anxiety, depression, and addictions to anything that makes them feel good about themselves. The men and the stories, the vulnerability they share with me has changed me. We will talk more about this in future chapters, but it's a callout to anyone wanting to make a difference for others and for themselves.

As I left, I couldn't get either out of my mind, so I reached out to simply see what the webinar was all about, left phone numbers for the young men I was mentoring, just in case they needed me, and then headed out on the journey of a lifetime, the journey that changed my life.

Three Key Signposts Along the Road to Purpose

1. Life isn't always fair, but life is, in fact, life. Learn from it.
2. Your past does not necessarily inform your future.
3. Hey, if you have lost a part of you, take time to grieve. It's okay to not be okay.

Chapter 2

Get Out Of Your Own Way

*"Only when we're brave enough to explore the darkness
will we discover the infinite power of our light."*

—Dr. Brené Brown

While I didn't know it then, I was standing in my own way. I was the only one who could change my destiny, yet I couldn't see it for the trees. After all, it was my company's fault that I was where I was. It was my age that kept me from getting those brewery jobs; it was anger with myself that I didn't take the easy way out so many years ago and go home to run my family businesses.

My very first experience with getting out of my own way started long before I ever gassed up the car. My greatest fear had always been being rejected, not being accepted, and in turn, being alone. I don't know where that comes from because people, friends, and family have always surrounded me. Maybe it was my habit of really getting attached to the people I loved and the trauma I faced when they had to leave. Grandparents as a kid, later best friends for another town, or later as an adult when I would change cities and work teams for new opportunities.

I'm not sure why, but I do know that it most likely impacted me. What I do know is that the series of events leading up to my trip had me on high alert that I was going to be alone. How on earth was I ever going to get a job at age 50, especially one that came anywhere close to the salary and benefits that 30 years of work had provided?

This fear was not without merit. In my corporate life, with two Fortune 100 companies, I had seen many talented people laid off or reorganized out of a job. Some never fully recovered. I had told myself that I never wanted that to happen to me. Unemployed at 50 was a worst-case scenario and something to be avoided at all costs. Because of that, I had worked diligently to stay ahead of technology and in the game. Nonetheless, given the lackluster response to the resumes I had submitted, I was fearful of the loss, that my lifestyle was going to change dramatically. In my mind, the voices added insult to injury: If I couldn't be who I was, I would be rejected and, in turn, alone in the world.

At least I knew I wouldn't be alone for the first part of the trip. My wife would be with me through our stop at her brother's home in Charlotte and sisters' homes in Tampa, along with a few unplanned stops along the way.

The first part of the trip was especially helpful because it gave us a lot of time to talk, just the two of us in the car, and with me in one of my most vulnerable states. I had told myself that I was the breadwinner in the family, and if I couldn't support my own family, what value did I bring? Our conversations were nothing short of grace; the support and encouragement that I usually supplied were now being provided to me.

My wife would be very patient and often reminded me that she was my biggest cheerleader even when my depression relieved itself through anger and self-pity. Her constant encouragement of, "you got this," "go on your trip and figure it out," "we will be fine" became the fuel for the trip. It helped a lot, knowing that this was all coming from someone who was not usually a big risk-taker.

As the tour progressed, my wife and I would talk each night, and at the suggestion of a friend, I would share pictures and comments from the road through Instagram. The funny part about this suggestion was that I had not used Instagram before the trip. Today, I find it ironic that the last-minute advice on an unlikely platform later became the diary for my entire trip. Neither the trip nor documenting it was ever a part of the plan, but was that one practice that has become the foundation for this book.

I packed up the car with what little I would need for who knows how long, and we headed east with no intended path but the first-night destination at my brother-in-law's house in Charlotte. My mind raced. *"I've never done this before. Never set out on a journey with no end in mind. I've never randomly walked away from responsibilities. Never ran away at all. What am I doing?"* I would just drive until it was time to find a place to eat or sleep.

I love eating and had put on the pounds in the three months since that fateful day in January, so our first stop was, of course, to eat, feed my stress. That first stop just happened to be Corbin, Kentucky, home of Colonel Sanders, the founder of Kentucky Fried Chicken. The little roadside diner was nothing like the restaurants that the global food giant owns all over the world today. The town was small, didn't have a lot of traffic, and there was only one other car in the cracked and dingy parking lot with faded lines, oil stains, and signs that once signaled the hottest thing in roadside dining so many years ago.

Inside, it was like a small bingo hall with a typical kitchen and dining counter, the original restaurant now a museum and attached to a more familiar but outdated KFC counter serving the same chicken found everywhere around the world. We would stop for lunch and a photo next to the life-size replica of the colonel that sat in the lobby. You may ask why Corbin and why KFC. Well, no reason. We saw the sign on the road and stopped in. That would become a theme of the journey that was ahead: see a sign, stop in. After all, I had no place to be and a lot of time to get there.

Early on in the journey, my anger had turned to sarcasm, and I had surrendered to negative thoughts, blame, and excuses, which would usually come out as dark sarcasm. My impression from this first stop raced through my head and ended in my very first post on Instagram.

Returning to the road to purpose:

Birthplace of Kentucky Fried Chicken and quadruple bypass surgery in Corbin, KY, was at odds with a glimmer of hope knowing that the Colonel was 65 when he started his company.

This stop had me thinking, *if this man could try and fail and try and fail and keep working and keep failing until he finally hit it big at 65, then maybe I could too.* Looking back now, what I learned on this stop was that, often, growth comes from being pushed beyond what was once comfortable. What was a sure thing, I would later discover, was that the very thing holding me back all along was my own limiting beliefs. I thought to myself, *How long has this been with me, how long have I been limiting myself?*

I had grown up feeling pretty average, nothing special, just a normal kid. So, my reaction was to never really push myself beyond what I felt an average kid was capable of: sports average, grades average, girls average, all parts of growing up never really feeling that I deserved more than average. While comforting at the time, as an adult, it was now keeping me from being my very best at work and in my relationships, and soon, it was coming full circle in a life without certainty. I thought to myself, *Had my career ended because I was average in an above-average company? Why was it that any time I got close to success, I would sabotage myself or give credit to someone else when I was the one who did the work?*

Now I know it was because of this belief that I was average. If I was to go anywhere, I needed to free my mind of the fear and self-doubt I had stored up for so long. I needed to learn to believe in myself again and own that I was not average and never had been.

This first stop on the journey I know now was never about the first stop. It was never about KFC or Corbin, Kentucky. It had no particular meaning at all but simply symbolized that I had taken the trip in the first place. That I had stepped outside my safe, over-planning, risk-averse, average self and made the first step. That first step would lead to other random and spontaneous first steps that spanned almost two months and launched what would become the most incredible years of my life.

The thing about corporate life or college life is that it is relatively comfortable. You pretty much know the playbook and what's going to happen next. You conform to the person you feel you should be at the time in the situations you find yourself. You keep your head down and avoid making waves to protect yourself and your position. The very thing that provides comfort is most likely holding us all back from realizing our destiny, especially when it comes to knowing yourself.

Sometimes, learning something about ourselves is uncomfortable. It often takes a smack in the face for us to stop and realize that while we may be focusing on the positive, those not-so-positive aspects of ourselves are holding us back in our relationships and our careers, keeping us from living up to our full potential. Our minds tell us stories from time to time, and in the crazy confusion of life, they go unnoticed by those around us. We know that in those stories, we feel like frauds even as we are moving forward. It doesn't feel right to be progressing in our minds. "I don't deserve to progress," is often a mantra that plays over and over again. In turn, while we are progressing, it takes a lot of effort. It's exhausting physically and draining emotionally. We often approach burnout and consider giving up, yet we keep pushing forward. It's that place, at that very moment that you feel a half step off, that you know that it shouldn't be as hard as it is. It is at precisely that moment that we need to keep pushing through. It is this very moment that inspires us to reflect on where we have been and why we chose the path we are on in the first place. One little setback, and we question our entire life.

For me, the sudden and unexpected career-changing move by my company had me questioning everything I thought I knew about myself. The top performer, the good guy, the leader who inspired ordinary people to do extraordinary things was now fighting off depression and the self-doubt that followed. My mindset had created a level of vulnerability that I was not accustomed to in my previous life. Yet the love and support of family and friends, especially those who refused to let me quit or feel sorry for myself, helped me move forward.

For those of us who always made things right, fixed ideas, and helped others, allowing those very same people to return the favor is difficult. I know you know what I am talking about if you too have ever experienced a difficult transition. Looking back, I now believe that those voices, those internal conversations to be nothing short of pure evil in our lives. It is evil keeping us from living the life we were born to live. Just think, if we were intended to live our best life, what would evil try to do? Keep us from living it.

So why is it that the most significant barrier between our success and happiness turns out to be ourselves? Well, simply put, fear, and those voices, those limiting beliefs. Compelling emotions that, if allowed to go unchecked, will keep us safe, average, comfortable, and mediocre. In the end, they will keep us from living the life we were meant to live. If we are to move forward, we need to overcome both. Let's take a little closer look at each of these great evils that hold us all back.

Overcoming Self-Limiting Beliefs

For me, the first of these two great evils is self-limiting beliefs. They are the cumulation of beliefs that are born in us through the conversations we have with ourselves brought on through our experiences and judgments made by the people in our life. For me, it has never been as much about the words but more about the example set by incredible people doing incredible things and never feeling quite like I ever measured up.

For me, this manifested in me telling myself that my struggle with weight was something I was born with or that I wasn't athletic, that I was lazy, and in turn, not good at sports. Or spending my entire life feeling average and never letting myself attempt to take on challenges that I thought only above-average people could accomplish.

For others, it might be economic beliefs like, "I'll never be successful in business because I come from a family that was never wealthy." Or a student who believes they can never go to college because no one in their family has. Or the young professional who understands that "I will never get the promotion because the glass ceiling keeps me down," and on and on. Is it the circumstance that is holding us back, or is it the excuses we make, the stories we tell ourselves, and how we are reacting to them? You know that those words shared with you as a child were out of love and support. But often, those same words hold you back today.

It is said that 85 percent of what's holding us back is "us," our thoughts, beliefs, and fears. Things that we have learned over a lifetime that may or may not still ring true. Something that you have learned, I have learned, we all have learned from growing up and the environments we experience along the way.

On the other hand, 15 percent of what's holding us back are the things that are entirely out of our control. This includes factorrs like the economy, the weather, or how others respond to us, external variables that no matter how much we would like to control the situation or other responses, we can't.

If we are reorganized, downsized, laid off, or let go for any other non-performance reason, then that is out of our control. If you don't get a job out of college or had to sit out a semester because the economy has experienced a downturn limiting both jobs and the ability to earn income, there's not much you can do about that either.

As hard as it might be, as much as it stokes the fires of insecurity in our brains, we should not spend one minute worrying about the things we cannot control. What can you do about it, anyway? When we blame others or make excuses, we are turning over all of our control to the situation or person who caused us pain. Trying to control the uncontrollable leads to depression, low self-esteem, and a feeling of not having control of our own lives. However, while we may not be able to control the situation, we can control how we react to it, how we judge it, and what we are going to do about it. Focusing on what we can control (ourselves) puts the control back in our hands versus delegating it to the situation or person or whatever else that caused the pain.

Philosophers have known this for centuries. Every dominant religion, the field of psychology, self-help gurus, and coaches have applied this very notion of focusing on what we can control and letting go of what we can't. Great laws have been established to explain the impact on our brain by this kind of thinking; modern-day neuroscience has proven it to be true. Concepts like "the law of attraction" say that you get what you think about most of the time. If you think about what you want and how to get it, guess what? You get it.

All successful people believe this way. They visualize success, set goals to achieve their visions, are optimistic, and believe in their ability to get what they want. They take personal responsibility and do the work. If they stumble, they pick themselves back up, learn, and try again. They believe that life is happening for them, not to them, and that failure is just another form of feedback.

You know these people; they are a joy to be around. They have higher levels of self-esteem and confidence than most people, and they generally enjoy life more. Simply being around them helps you see the world in the same way. Taking responsibility for your success is critical, especially during a difficult transition to move forward. Are you moving forward? Do you think about that new job you want, and are you willing to do the work, build the resume, acquire the new skills, and do whatever it takes? If so, you will find that you will get precisely that: what you want. You become a victor and embrace a life that is happening for you.

Unsuccessful people, on the other hand, think about what they are trying to avoid, what they don't want, and guess what they get? Exactly: what they don't want. They blame others, make excuses, and hold on to past grudges and thoughts of inadequacy brought on by mistakes of the past. They fail to forgive and forget and get on with their lives. They are negative, and they believe that life is happening to them. They are angry, often unhappy, and, most times, depressed. So, are you thinking about the low-paying job you don't want, starting over at an entry-level role, or becoming a greeter at a big chain store? Stop it!

For me, these ideas about mindset proved to be true. My thought was precisely on that: what I didn't want. I didn't want to be unemployed. I didn't want to be looking for something new at 50 years old. I didn't want to start all over at a much lower salary. By focusing on what I didn't want, being 50+ and out of work, that is what I got: being 50+ and out of work. By holding on to anger, blaming my past company, not forgiving the people I trusted, or using my age as an excuse, I quickly spiraled to hell and found myself angry, depressed, and void of any kind of self-confidence needed to persevere. I had created a thought in my mind that life was happening to me and, in so doing, became a victim of my own life choices. I was thinking about what I didn't want, and guess what I got? Exactly what I didn't want.

For me, the early stops along the road to purpose gave me the time to empty my head of the anger, blame, and excuses and own the fact that the decisions made that placed me on the road to purpose in the first place were out of my control. Not a thing I could do about it. What I learned was that my reaction to the situation, not the situation itself, was keeping me from healing. I focused on being angry, placing blame, or holding grudges instead of doing what I should be doing, like getting my resume polished up and focusing on getting a new job. When I changed my thinking after long days on the road, things began to change. A glimmer of light at the far end of a very long tunnel was starting to reveal itself.

Coincidently, I saw the same thing happening with the young men that I mentored, and when they started focusing on what they could control, guess what? Things improved. When they concentrated on getting good grades and working to put themselves through school, it didn't matter that they came from

families that were economically challenged or had never dreamed of attending college. The road to purpose taught me to focus on what we can control and that it is up to us to choose success and then do the work to bring it to life.

Many of today's leading psychologists' research confirms this notion. Leaders in their fields include Dr. Martin Seligman, Dr. Carol Dweck, and Angela Duckworth, who studied the power of optimism, mindset, and resilience, and more. I will introduce these incredible thinkers to you later in the book. Their work has transformed the way I see success and our ability to determine our destiny through our own thinking. Learning from this research, along with my own experiences, taught me that nothing could get in the way of our success but us. That whatever happened in the past, those stupid things that we did or evil things that happened to us, not a thing can stop you but you. That where we come from has nothing to do with where we can go. That the only time we fail is when we quit.

For the first time, I decided to do something unplanned. At first, it was slow and easy, with my wife by my side. I asked myself what I had to lose and pushed past that comfort zone, and guess what? I survived. I took baby steps first and got used to pushing boundaries.

For me, that was our stop in Asheville, North Carolina. It was early on, and I was still holding on to what I knew: beer. Even though my attempts to work for a craft brewer had been in vain, there I was amongst them in a city known for its craft beer industry. I was definitely in my comfort zone on this stop, and if I was being sarcastic, it came out in the conversation I was having with myself that day.

Returning to the road to purpose:

Now that is more like it! The road to purpose found me thinking "beer" in Asheville, what I knew best and what had given me a successful corporate life. I now know what I found was my comfort zone, my safe place, my prison that was keeping me from living my full potential. What I have learned is that success, happiness, and living one's best life often travels through a series of events, often painful and always an opportunity to learn. A trip that requires courage to overcome self-limiting beliefs and push forward. A journey that begins the transformation to become all you were created to be. Asheville, NC

What I have learned along the journey that followed is that if you can learn self-limiting beliefs, then you can also unlearn them. The secret, wait for it, is merely pushing ourselves into places that make us uncomfortable, places where if we approached and conquered would most likely give us an elevated self-image and, in turn, success. We need to simply ask ourselves, "What is the absolute worst thing that could happen to me if I attempt it?" If you can live with that worst-case scenario, then make your move and simply have the courage to try to make small steps. Create small wins at first to get you past this uncomfortable place. You will soon find yourself well on your own way to the success and prosperity that you are looking for. To do this, you must be willing to stumble, to fall, to make mistakes, and yes, to fail, learn, and try again. To never give up.

I learned this, and I bet if you look back on your life, you did too. Ask yourself, when you focused your mind on achieving a goal and did the work, did you achieve it? It has been a mindset that got me past those who doubted me or thought I was overly optimistic about an outcome. It was often a mindset that took limited resources, found innovative ways to approach a problem, and returned record results. Today, it is a mindset that ensures that I focus on my purpose every day to help my clients achieve their full potential.

So, what's holding you back? How do you explain the negative things that happen to you in your life? Do you see the world as an opportunity or a threat? What are the voices in your head telling you? Do you believe them? Are there any facts to back them up, or are they just thoughts?

Finding Courage and Facing Fear

Well, if self-limiting beliefs had an evil first cousin, it would have to be fear. At one point in human history, it was fear that kept us alive and saved us from being eaten by wild animals before modern conveniences protected us from our environments. Now it keeps us from being our very best. So, what are you afraid of?

Fear and its sidekick, anger, are the two most powerful emotions. Some say they're twice as powerful as love. Humans are programmed to do just two things: seek pleasure and avoid pain. Pain is that fear, the fear of losing something. Fear of loss or rejection: not smart enough, sexy enough, rich enough, not enough? Fear of failure. What if it doesn't work? I could lose everything. Fear of being average or ordinary, and get this: fear of success. Which one keeps you from being your very best?

To understand fear, we must first understand that our brains can attempt to divert us from pain, discomfort, or stress. For most of us, our mind stops us at somewhere around 40 percent of our total capacity. That's 60 percent that we are not taking advantage of to achieve our full potential. So why not push it a little? What do you have to lose if you give it a shot? Strangely, we hold ourselves back through this fear. We know that staying where we are is not providing happiness, yet we fear to do something else.

I have learned this in my own life, and it has changed me. If you want a second opinion, meet Dr. Martin Seligman, father of the field of Positive Psychology and professor at the University of Pennsylvania. He studied and wrote extensively on "learned helplessness" and proves this notion of giving up when things get uncomfortable. In his studies, he found that lab animals simply accept pain when they feel that they have no control over it, and they make no effort to move away from the source of the pain. Do we humans do the same with what is comfortable? Have we learned that moving past what we know is going to produce pain, so why bother? Or is that simply our minds telling us that it could happen, our brains protecting our bodies from what it expects will be painful? Why do we allow our brains to think in this way? Have we been programmed to do so?

My next stop would remind me of what can happen when you simply push yourself past the fear of failure. With Asheville in the rearview mirror, our next stop landed us in Charlotte, North Carolina, with my brother-in-law Jeff and his family.

Jeff, a determined, driven man, was successful in every way. He had experienced much success and failure in his life, yet he never stopped moving forward. Jeff was the guy that, at the height of a lucrative media career, decided to venture out on his own and make his destiny. He was a man who knew no strangers. A person who could identify a problem and provide a solution that gave his clients a better life. Jeff could walk into a room and walk out with a new friend or appointment to further his business. He had worked for large companies and put it all on the line to start his own business.

While I didn't know it at the time, that was precisely the way I needed to start this trip, with a man who had set aside the comfort of a lucrative career to do his own thing, to start his own business. Jeff would reinforce my decision to go out on my own at this stop, saying that he had no doubt I would be successful. He told me that it was going to take a lot of work but that hadn't been a problem for him. Seeing Jeff in particular during this time of great fear and self-doubt reminded me that success was really up to me, and at that moment, I needed that more than anything else. The stop in Charlotte was a perfect kick-off to the trip and would set the pace for self-discovery in the days that followed. My post from that day helped bring that to life for me.

Returning to the road to purpose:

James Taylor's "Carolina in my Mind" danced in my head as I entered his home state. What I found on this part of the trip was that, sometimes, the things we are looking for are right out in front of us in the things we might take for granted.

Family is one of those things: our foundation by which we build our castle on as we go through life. We start with the family we are born with, then add in all the people who love us for who we are, push us to be our best selves, celebrate with us, and console us when we need it. Our friends, family, and those we volunteer with, work with and, in turn, the ones who change our world.

Those people who sometimes come into our lives at precisely the right time for the right reason, though what that reason is is often unexplainable. They are the family that we choose (or choose us) along the way. Both, together, make building that castle of our lives possible. Charlotte, NC

What I learned in Charlotte was that fear of failure or rejection is only something to be afraid of when you quit. You are not growing if you are not failing, and that seems like the most significant loss of all to me. When fear takes over, try this quick mind hack: Replace the word "failure" with "feedback," and you will soon move past fear toward your destiny. You see, when you fail and learn, you don't fail at all. You simply make the changes and move on. Getting past the fear of failure often takes courage and requires you to take action in the face of fear, so push past your comfort zone to find the growth you desire.

Life Is How We Judge It

So far, we have talked about those thoughts and fears that hold us back from achieving our best self. We pondered what they were and how they got in our heads. We have talked about action being the answer to overcoming those fears and limiting beliefs. Oftentimes, it is merely changing the way that we see things, how we judge the situation that needs to change. Being spontaneous in thoughts, like actions, will help us understand things differently.

How we see the world is how we get the world. Do we have an optimistic view, a hopeful outlook, or a contrary view, a cynical view? What are the words we use? "Can," "will," "am?" Or, "can't," "hope to," "might"? How we talk to ourselves is essential, and approaching things from an optimistic viewpoint is critical if we want to bring success into our lives. Experts in the field have studied this behavior for decades and, for the most part, come to similar conclusions that when one feels optimistic about their own life, they tend to get the results they want.

Dr. Carol Dweck, professor of psychology and author of the book *Mindset,* defines this theory by identifying two types of mindsets. The first is a fixed mindset where we accept what is happening to us as just the way it is. The second type of mindset is growth, or the notion that we are in control of our infinite ability or believe that life is happening for us. It's an optimistic outlook on one's life. Her research found that the growth mindset is where happiness and success come together.

Dr. Martin Seligman (who we talked about earlier) also discovered that if you could learn helplessness, then you could also learn to be optimistic. He found that seldom is it the situation itself that is causing you problems but rather how you judge the experience that drives mindset. In other words, do you define conditions in your life as permanent or temporary? For example, if you are a student and you fail a test, do you describe yourself as stupid, a permanent descriptor? Or do you say to yourself, "maybe I should study more next time," which reflects more of a temporary mindset?.

If you've been laid off or retired from your current job, do you say to yourself, "I'm unemployable," or do you explain the situation as an opportunity to pursue the passions that you have always wanted to pursue? In both examples, which are reactions to a challenging life circumstance, we have the chance to view the experience in a positive, permanent way or a temporary, negative way. The good news is we can learn to take the optimistic view.

Dr. Seligman and Dr. Dweck found that optimism is key to a happy and fulfilling life. When you see yourself in control of your own life, you are more content, positive, and optimistic about reaching your full potential. If you see negative situations as temporary and you approach life through the lens of possibility and growth, then you will do what it takes to learn from setbacks and try again until you achieve your goals and your vision of your best life. The secret to success came full circle as we left Charlotte and could be pulled together in a simple phrase: Go for it. What do you have to lose?

Returning to the road to purpose:

Be spontaneous from time to time, enjoy the unknown, venture out, and do something for no reason but to know you can. So many of life's treasured moments are unplanned. Go for it!

"Spontaneous Greg" chooses a Savannah brewpub for lunch, "planning Greg" didn't realize it was March 17 in the city with the second-largest St. Pats celebration in the country! And the hundreds of thousands who choose to celebrate there. "May the road rise to meet you."

Savannah, GA

I definitely would not advise choosing Savannah for lunch on St. Patrick's Day. Unless, of course, you are there to celebrate St. Patrick's Day. One thing that I have found for sure is that if given a chance to overthink something, I'm going to do it. The more I dwell on a tough decision, the more likely I am to talk myself out of it. Do you see the same in yourself? Given a chance, if we give our brain time enough, it will find a way to stop us from moving forward, especially on those emotionally charged decisions that have perceived consequences before we try them out.

What I learned on this portion of the trip is that, often, there is no plan. Sometimes you just go for it for no reason at all. Logic would have stopped me from taking this trip, and had that happened, none of the life experiences that followed would have come to be.

What I discovered during this part of the trip was that the first step is knowing yourself and, in particular, knowing what has been holding you back. For me, it was the subconscious idea that I was average and how that incited the fear of pursuing or doing anything that I perceived was beyond ordinary. I learned that what was keeping me from living my full potential was inside of me and could be unlearned, that our lives and control over our outcomes are within our power to change.

I learned that the first step is to learn to overcome these self-imposed barriers and get on to achieving our most significant goals on the way to a life we have never allowed ourselves to believe was possible. You can do this very same thing on your transition by taking control of your thoughts, removing self-limiting beliefs, and embracing an optimistic mindset.

So, how do we do that?

First, we have to understand that our brain's role first and foremost is to protect our bodies from those things that could do us harm. It's also important to note that our mind, while a beautiful organ that can store all of the experiences of our lives, can only process one thought at a time, and the default is always a cautious one. If we can replace that negative thought with a positive one, then we are well on our way to achieving the attitude needed for success.

Second, live your purpose. Knowing why we exist, what drives our very existence, and how we use it to bring value to other people creates a sense that everything is as it should be. We are happier, our self-image improves, and everything else seems to fall into place.

Third, believe in yourself. Remember that brain of ours that is always trying to protect us? This is often taught to us by people who are trying to protect us. We learn that we should approach life with caution through words like "no," "don't," "can't," "average," words that keep us from venturing outside our comfort zone. As adults, these words come back to us as "self-limiting beliefs," especially when we're under pressure. That can, in turn, create self-doubt and a feeling that we are not in control of our own lives.

Fourth, the great news is that if we can learn self-limiting beliefs, then we can also unlearn them. A great way to do this is through a simple self-talk exercise. Athletes often call it "psyching yourself up" before that big game, or that important presentation, or the final exam, or asking that person out on a date, or any other time you are required to operate outside your comfort zone. By simply saying to yourself something like, "I am proud of myself," "I can do this," or, "I am responsible for my own *success"* over and over, your mind begins to reprogram the negative thoughts with positive ones.

Fifth, if our mind can only process one thing at a time, positive thinking doesn't allow a place for negative thoughts to fester. Eventually, our attitude changes from *"can't"* to *"can."* We muster the courage to take action, which more times than not results in, at the very least, learning. Success breeds success, and confidence improves. Try it; you will be amazed at how powerful this tip can be.

Three Key Signposts Along the Road to Purpose

1. Identify your limiting beliefs and what holds you back, and put them behind you.
2. Overcoming fear starts with being afraid and doing it anyway. Find courage.
3. Life is how you view it; all successful people see life optimistically.

Chapter 3

Mountains And Speed Bumps

"Fail early, fail often, but always fail forward."

—John Maxwell

A theme had set in at this point on the journey. I had been holding myself back almost all my life. That fear, those limiting beliefs, and those voices in my head would kick in every time I was up against a challenge or an opportunity, a mountain of sorts that stood between where I was in life and where I wanted to be. Like most mountains, they can seem daunting at first looking up from the base just before a climb. *How am I going to get to the other side?* is the question for some that make the climb not worth the effort. After all, I was not a mountain climber.

What I learned on the journey was a new perspective, a new way of looking at the mountains in my way. Seeing the challenge as it is, thinking of ways to get around it, believing that you can, and then taking the first step, then the next, and the next. That was all it took to get past the fear and limiting beliefs that had kept me from the summit for so long. Like climbing a mountain, we get to the top by taking each step, and when we do, we enjoy the very best views that often come from reaching the summit.

I had faced many mountains in my life that had usually resulted in a loss of some kind, damage to status, loss of opportunity, or people leaving my life. Things like not getting that job I never applied for because I didn't believe I would get it or that breakup after a long engagement with a past fiancé when I hesitated to make the final commitment of marriage. Or when I passed up the opportunity to work overseas because of the fear that it would disrupt my family or leave me stuck in a foreign land if it didn't work out. In school, it was not becoming the architect or mechanical engineer because I didn't think I could pass the math classes required to accel in the field. The situation I was in now was no different, yet it felt like a mountain that I just didn't have the energy to climb. The thoughts of regaining my position in life felt daunting. I contemplated that *maybe I just need to pitch my tent, accept my lot in life, and camp at the foot of this mountain, resigning myself to what could have been.*

I'm sure you have been at exactly this place in life. If you're a young person, how many times have you not gone out for the sport because you didn't think you were talented enough? How many times have you not asked that particular person out on a date because you thought that they might say no? How about that job you didn't apply for because you thought others were a better fit? Over 50 is no different. Often, we stay in a job because the money is too good to leave or give up that dream to own our own business because it's just too risky. After all, well, we could fail at it. We miss all these opportunities because we let ourselves use the mountain as an excuse. We give in to the struggle before we ever make the first step.

Here is what I learned during this part of the road to purpose: While we may not be able to control the size of the mountain, we can control how we approach the mountain. It's just a choice, and we are in control of the choices we make. We relate to this because our lives are, for the most part, a series of mountains, ups and downs, peaks and valleys. We all face times when we are up against a "decisive crisis" that we must overcome to grow and move on with our life.

I liken this to hiking a trail and approaching a mountain that stands in our way. Being 50 and out of work was like that to me as I approached the tall and rugged face that was now before me, not knowing how I would get past it. Often, we must approach the mountains in our lives, those seemingly insurmountable challenges that we must face to transform and grow. Like the hike to the summit, once achieved, we get a glimpse of the entire range. As in life, the view from the top is a fantastic sight to be seen and makes the challenge seem less daunting as the mountain range gets smaller and smaller out into infinity. The more mountains we climb, the easier it becomes turning what was once in our way, a barrier to our success, into a speed bump. You know it's there, but it just slows you down for a while on your own way to achieving your destiny.

For me, leaving my corporate life after 30 years without an understanding of what the future would bring felt like the end of my life, an insurmountable mountain of sorts. I was 50 years old, highly compensated, and out of work. My mind was full of thoughts like, "Who is going to hire a 50-year-old, especially one in my pay range?" I was angry, scared, and felt as if all that I had worked for over the past 30 years was for naught. My self-worth, self-esteem, and self-image were gone—a failure at 50, my final chapter.

I was on the verge of giving up when I had a thought: *I had faced mountains before.* For the most part, challenging as they were, I had lived through them and am still here today to share the story. My "mountains," like losing my first job out of school with a startup that didn't make it, spawned a depression and sense of worthlessness that followed. Or my first engagement, which ended in months of crying, debilitating sadness, missed work, and isolation from friends but made room for new people in my life, including my wife of over 25 years. For me, it took counseling at precisely the right time to help me take the first step in getting over those mountains of my past.

What breaks my heart, though, are the mountains that the young people I met along the road to purpose are facing. Many are suffering, especially the young men who I have mentored after returning from the journey. They are unbeaten in every way yet empty inside. They have no experience to fall back on to let them know that they too will make it over their mountains.

Those mountains often find young people in very dark places, including suicide and substance abuse. I go to bed each night and wake up each morning thinking about how I can make a dent in this epidemic of sadness in our young people today. I often find myself in tears, overwhelmed by knowing that one in four young people are suffering from a mental health crisis because of what seems like a hopeless case to fit in. It has become my calling, and the reason why has been made clear since the trip. It is in these young men that I found inspiration to share some of my most vulnerable times, my biggest mountains that I had held deep inside all my life, with the young men I mentor.

One exceptional young man, after a breakup with a long-time girlfriend, felt unlovable and unworthy of life instead of seeing the opportunity to meet and find the partner of his dreams. For another, a series of failed exams left him believing that he was "stupid" instead of him merely telling himself he had to study more the next time. Or another young man, a fantastic talent with a massive heart, who saw himself as "not enough" to do even the most basic of tasks, fearing a life of failure, loss of those he loved, and loneliness, all the while always finishing at the top of his class. He was loved by all who knew him.

A vast majority of the young people I work with describe bad things in their life as permanent, and that has led to double-digit growth of suicides in this age group and, by the way, in my 50+ age group as well. Suicide is now only second to accidents as the leading cause of death for young people.

Just before I left on my trip, a young man in the organization I work with hung himself over the holiday break. He was a shining light for all those who knew him yet hid a dark spot deep inside himself, not to burden his friends. A year later, another who had graduated four years prior said goodbye to his girlfriend as he sat on a train track and was run over by a train. Two others made attempts but were saved by their friends, true heroes, just in time.

Suicide amongst young, hyper-talented people breaks my heart more than anything I have ever experienced. Our young people today cannot see the speed bumps on the other side of the mountain. They just aren't resilient and often give up with the first sign of loss. They need our help.

Why is this that they are so vulnerable to life's challenges? One theory is that as we became more affluent and have used that affluence to provide for our children, we, in turn, overprotected them. Today as young adults, they have never experienced failure and have no idea how to recover from the inevitable bad that will visit their lives from time to time. I liken it to the analogy that "we never let them climb trees, let alone learn how to pick themselves back up after they fell out of one." We must help them, and in so doing, ourselves become resilient. Later on in the book, I will share this experience and make a case for mentorship as a way to build relationships and resiliency in both the young and the not-so-young who mentor them.

Grit and Grace

The road to purpose went through many towns along the way that could have been named "Resilience" because that is what those stops brought to life through the many people I met. Resilient people who had been through the worst that life had to give, yet stood firm, filled with faith, and were able to move on despite the trauma and pain they had experienced. Being resilient is not something we are born with, hope for, or that comes as part of our ordinary lives. Being resilient is something we learn through facing unexpected uncertainty and pain and moving through it. I know that we will be okay even when, at times, it doesn't feel like it will ever end. Resilience is not something we hope for or want to have happened to us; it is something we must decide to be. Like so many things along the road to purpose, taking ownership of my own decisions is what made the difference.

I'm no superhero. Often, I was required to suck it up and just do it because I had no other choice due to circumstances out of my control and, in so doing, became more resilient. Deciding to be resilient is seldom an easy task. My experience has been that when the world seemed to fall apart all around me, I had two choices: deal with it or surrender. Out of work at 50+ was one of those times. I had two options: retire and fade into the past or step up, get over myself, and get on with it. My time in Florida had me asking myself, *Would I simply fade into the past or push on to chart a new future?*

Returning to the road to purpose:

Stop number five was Tampa, Florida, to visit my wife's sister's family. Tampa would be the last stop before she would grab a plane back home, and I would venture west with no particular destination in mind. This family, in particular, my brother-in-law and I, had worked together over 25 years ago. He had introduced my wife to me, and as it turned out, she had asked me to a company bowling party. As the story goes, I agreed to go to the party with her if she would go to a banquet for a group we sponsored where I was to accept an award for 25 years' support of the organization on behalf of my company. Well, both of those events were comical, and 25 years later, she is still the love of my life.

That in mind, my brother-in-law and I reminisce about who could keep up when it came to drinking beer. Well, 25 years later, and I am still trying. What I have learned since then is that all things happen for a reason: the good, the bad, and the times you never think you will survive. It's recognizing those things and holding on tight that can be the biggest challenge, yet they're the ones that stitch together the beauty that is the fabric of our lives. Tampa, FL

My time in Tampa would be the starting point of ups and downs on the rollercoaster of the first half of my trip. As I was preparing to leave, my brain was in high gear, overthinking everything.

What was I doing? I thought, *I have responsibilities. People are counting on me. Am I letting them down? Am I running away from reality?* Self-doubt battled with adventure. I was holding on to the past while dreaming of a better future. Responsibility versus irresponsibility?

Returning to the road to purpose:

Today was the day. Donna flew home, and I left the security of the family. Today I would spend the next couple of months by myself in a car between stops. Unplanned, random, and alone. Could someone who had spent his entire life with others learn to be alone with himself for hours on end? That scared the hell out of me. One thing's for sure, you learn to like yourself and soon realize you're not a bad guy. What I know now is that you must learn to love yourself before you can truly love others. The next few weeks would be learning to do just that. Fun is FAMILY. Palm Harbor, FL

Love is an awesome wife who sends you off on the journey of a lifetime.

It took Margaritaville's Landshark Landing (an old and loyal friend from my past) to remind me to "Escape the Everyday," the everyday of self-limiting beliefs, as I hugged the Florida Gulf Coast and ran into an old friend at my first lunch stop... hello Landshark! Changes in latitudes, changes in attitudes at Landshark Landing, Pensacola, FL.

What I learned on this part of the trip is that you must decide to be resilient. For me, that meant being very clear on what I wanted to do and why I wanted to do it. Next, embrace the virtue of excellence, be more forgiving of yourself and others, and see the beauty inside of you no matter what. Then we must own our reality, confront it, and accept "what is" with hope for what tomorrow will bring. Then, as we have said before, nothing happens without the courage to take the first step, to stumble, learn, and get back up again. It's essential not to make the same mistake twice, to learn and make adjustments, to see each day as a new opportunity to grow and to ignore the critics that would hold you back.

So, what is true resilience? I mean to be resilient when the absolute worst of the worse happens? The next few days would take me along the southern coast to the far southern tip of Texas, then north to Oklahoma. It was in Texas and Oklahoma where I would experience resilience in its purest form through my visit with a set of cousins and their families who had been through a lifetime of pain and suffering and the lives they have lived despite it.

They had suffered insurmountable mountains yet found success, happiness, and faith in the aftermath. They managed to hold on to the best parts of the past and move forward, to be resilient when everything that matters was taken from them. I had grown up with this set of cousins, but it wasn't until the road to purpose that I realized that true resilience had been there right in front of me all my life. It wasn't until now that I truly understood the power this family, the light this family had been shining on the rest of us all along, the perfect example of true resilience, of faith, grit, and grace.

This set of cousins, two sisters and a brother, had seen it all, and my first stop in Texas was with the oldest, Kelli, an incredibly strong woman who held her family together at a very young age against incredible odds. Kelli would be the one who would step up and help her mother raise her two younger siblings during her parents' divorce and when child support ended. She would be the one who later had to bring the family back together to help her father manage through Lou Gehrig's disease and subsequently die from it. Kelli would be the older sister who later had to do the same when her mother would then die from cancer. Kelli would also be the one who ensured that she and her siblings never lost touch with my family, making every effort to participate in family gatherings and build the connections that would sustain them through some of the toughest of times.

Returning to the road to purpose:

The road to purpose would have me experiencing perseverance on many occasions but nothing like my stop in south Texas to visit my cousin Kelli. Kelli, Mike, and family had moved around a lot with Mike's work as an engineer in the energy industry. They would eventually live in a town just south of Houston. The city was known for street signs that read "this way" or "that way," which ironically summed up my life at this point.

Cousin Kelli is an amazing woman in her own right. A person who never quit, no matter how challenging life got, she got things done. Today a successful woman in every way, with an awesome family and happy life, and the mother of two very talented and confident daughters who are on their way to changing the world.

What I learned on this stop is that family comes first (even for prodigal sons like me) and that being successful, being happy is all about "deciding to be" then doing the hard work to make it so and having a lot of fun along the way. I have been fortunate to be surrounded by strong, smart, and confident women all my life, women who pushed through it all and never gave up.

The best time was exploring South Texas with one of the strongest people I know, my cousin Kelli! Lake Jackson, TX

After a fantastic couple of days in South Texas, I loaded up the car and headed north. The anger had left me by this time, leaving me not fulfilled but empty. My time in Texas, though, had me thinking about what I was going to fill that "empty" space up with, and for the first time, I started thinking about the future and what my role would be in it.

The next stop was cousin Jeff's home in Tulsa. Jeff, the youngest brother of Kelli, had also pushed through all kinds of adversity that goes with being a young man growing up without a father. He always seemed to find "the fun" in almost everything, and like his dad, lived life to the fullest. He would eventually marry, start a beautiful family, and own a series of successful businesses. Jeff and I, of course, talked about business and my time with adult beverage companies. His mind was always working, and he shared a thought about a beverage business around the lake where he owned a second home. It was nice being confirmed for my experience, and it added a block of confidence to my new self. The youngest of cousins now helping the oldest cousin think about the second half of his life. It was in Tulsa where the first spark of an idea of business ownership would find its way into my thoughts.

We would also get a surprise visit from his and Kelli's sister Julie and her son Riley while I was there. Like her siblings, Julie had navigated the same challenging life and had gone on to be a successful businessperson in her own right. She had followed her dream and turned her passion for gymnastics into a career with a national company that supplied college and universities with equipment for cheerleading squads, Greek support merchandise, and much more. Riley, a very, very good baseball player, had just finished up his college career and was working with his Uncle Jeff. He also had a passion for playing the guitar and would later move to Nashville to pursue that dream of music. Julie's other son, Brock, was not with us that night. He was busy with a much higher calling and the catalyst for true resilience like one could never imagine.

Returning to the road to purpose:

Found me in Tulsa, OK, visiting my cousin Jeff, his family, and a surprise visit from his sister, Julie, my cousin, and her son Riley for the night from Dallas. My past life chasing corporate dreams often found me without time for friends, extended family, and others who were not part of the master plan of climbing that corporate ladder, a ladder I would later find was leaning against the wrong building.

Lessons learned on this part of the trip were many: 1. family and friends are there for you when you lose your own way, even when you are not there for them, 2. that life is fleeting and that people come and go from your life for a reason. That when your purpose here on earth is completed, God will take you back, and 3. that we can persevere and overcome incredible hardships and pain to realize our best selves.

For this family, hardship came from divorce and later the loss of both parents to ALS and cancer at a very young age. The loss of Brock: son, brother, nephew, to a horrible car accident at 16, a shooting star for our family, his friends, classmates, and all who knew him. Most, suffering this kind of pain, would have given up, but not this family. They grew closer, moved forward, and have realized success and happiness in every way: in business, in the family, in every way.

What I learned on this stop is that if my cousins could overcome their unimaginable pain to be the best they could be, then I could too. That resilience all started with facing those challenges and a decision to move past them. My cousin Julie left her boys each morning with the charge "Go Be Great," and they, all of them, approached the world in that very way, "great." And, in turn, they inspire us all to be the very best we can be no matter our circumstances. That life is not always easy. Through faith, each other, determination, and perseverance, we will pull through and live the life intended, a life of meaning and purpose.

That final night, my cousin's son Riley played the song "Wagon Wheel" in tribute to Brock, who had passed away a few years back from an auto accident at 16. Riley is now chasing his dream as he sang the words of that song by Darius Rucker, "So, rock me momma like a wagon wheel. Rock me, momma, any way you feel. Hey, momma rock me. Rock me momma like the wind and the rain. Rock me momma like a south-bound train. Hey, momma rock me."

Oklahoma was a special stop of perseverance. A living example of turning mountains into speed bumps. A place where once in a while, you get shown the light in the strangest of places if you look at it right! Tulsa, OK

This part of the journey would show me that life can be overbearing, and at times, it may feel like no matter how hard you try, it never quite ends up the way you intended. Where I started would prove this to be true over and over again. No matter how difficult the decision to push through the struggle, to persevere, that is what has always made the difference for me. That quitting was the only time you ever lose. That getting past the tough times is the only way to realize great times. Really, if we are honest with ourselves, great times need tough times to shine through. In the end, struggling to summit the mountains in our lives was the only way to see the incredible view that lay on the other side.

I often talk about speed bumps with the young people I mentor. I can remember as a young man when all of life's struggles felt like insurmountable mountains, mountains many young people face today without the luxury of time and experience to know that it will all work out in the end. Mountains like a breakup with your first love and wondering if you will never find love again, or flunking that first exam of your college career and questioning whether or not college was for you. What time and experience provide is learning is that with all the struggle, the mistakes and broken dreams, come growth. Growth from learning how to do things differently the next time. Growth from knowing how you react to the challenge and who is there to help you through it.

What I also learned is that the only time you fail is when you quit. That in pain is growth, and in growth often comes a life of success that most of us never permit ourselves to even dream of. What I learned was that where resilience and perseverance come together is where one can see the light at the end of the tunnel. As we climb to the top of the mountain, we see the beauty on the other side; we find the strength to survive failure and the determination to keep trying over and over again until we achieve our goal. Oftentimes, this comes from deep inside when we least expect it, like being called by something greater than ourselves. I have come to know this as "Grit and Grace."

Grit and grace are two words that I never thought would come out of my mouth in the same phrase. Grit, as I define it, is the ability to get down and dirty, do the hard stuff, outwork everyone else, and get it done no matter what. In her book, *Grit,* Angela Duckworth, Ph.D., defines grit as "passion and sustained persistence applied toward long-term achievement, with no particular concern for rewards or recognition along the way."

For me, grit is the ability to do whatever it takes without letting fear get in the way. That nagging fear of pissing someone off or chasing them away had always kept me from doing the challenging things. Then there was the fear of failing and, in turn, being rejected as a failure. Often, I would forgo a promotion or leave a position that I liked so that someone else, usually an employee or mentee, could have the slot. Often, instead of celebrating their success, I would end up with a nagging bitterness toward the very person I was "sacrificing for" in the name of earning their friendship. In turn, I would usually push that friendship away with the bitterness I would hold deep inside myself. It was often my actions that brought on the very loneliness that I was so afraid of.

Grace, on the other hand, are those gifts we receive that we don't deserve, that we didn't earn. For some, grace is a gift from the divine, the master of the universe, from God. For others, grace is what occurs when the mind finds flow, when results exceed expectations with little to no perceived effort. For me, grace has shown up in almost every difficult time in my life, often after a painful breakup or loss of some kind. You know, the kind of difficulties that make you want to say WTF and quit. Often at that very moment is when grace appears, usually after some form of sacrifice that caused you pain. For me, this generally shows up in the form of flow and plain old good luck.

I know you know what I am talking about, and you have most likely experienced the same when you were ready to throw in the towel and someone showed up to change your world, save your life, and help you see things differently. Grace is what found me along the journey. Grace is what smacked me in the face when I was angry for being out of work, blaming the people who made the calls. Before my journey, grace didn't exist. You earned it in the form of success. You worked for it, did whatever it took to gain it. God had nothing to do with it.

Well, the road to purpose changed all that for me. Something unexplainable filled the empty spot inside my own heart when I had nothing left to give, no meaning, no purpose, just empty. Not even anger could find a place inside me. Then it happened. My mind opened, and the answer I had been looking for was clear as day. Something lit that spark in my mind and put me in a place to accept grace. When I stopped fighting myself and my past and opened my heart to the universe, the universe gave back tenfold. For me, at my most vulnerable time, I know now that nothing short of God had a hand in it.

Everything Happens for a Reason

Somewhere between Oklahoma and New Mexico, alone with myself in the car with nothing more than XM radio to keep me company, Garth Brooks, the country music multi-platinum artist, came on the radio. Garth, a native of Oklahoma and favorite son, had been there for me a long time ago during one of those life struggles I had experienced when an engagement broke off after a long time with an incredible woman. That song, "The Dance," told the story of the pain of loss that is always possible and the notion that if we knew of the pain prior, we would never allow ourselves into the relationship in the first place. The chorus of the song, "I could have missed the pain, but I would have had to miss the dance," talks about the good times that would not have happened had you never gave the relationship a chance in the first place. A new perspective on focusing on joy versus the fear of pain.

Well, Garth was back on the radio again at precisely the right time with a new song, "Belleau Wood." In this song, he shares the notion that for those of us searching for answers, for hope, that may we need not look any further than having faith, and just maybe we are looking in the wrong place. He brings this thought to life in his lyric: *"But for just one fleeting moment. The answer seemed so clear; Heaven's not beyond the clouds, it's just beyond the fear. No, heaven's not beyond the clouds, it's for us to find it here."*

So, a second major life challenge, and Garth Brooks was right back there with me helping me sort through it all. Coincidence? You will have to decide for yourself, but for me, I now know it as grace.

Before the trip, I found myself at odds with organized religion. First, the faith I was raised in, then all organized religion. I had a problem with the agendas of some, the hypocrisy of others, and the judgment and exclusion of most. I had moved away from religion as a source of comfort. I continued to hold on to various teachings, but it had become more about respect for other people in my life who held religion close than it was for me. What I found on the road to purpose was that while organized religion was not on the top of my playlist, spirituality itself was quickly moving up the list. Today, I do align myself with traditional religious beliefs yet consider myself not to be very religious.

I wasn't alone in this struggle for answers. I met many people who were struggling with their grasp of religion and spirituality and questioning whether or not a higher power of any kind existed. I found many with the desire to believe in something bigger than themselves, something to provide hope for a better future and to know that what they do makes a difference. They want to know that who they are counts for something but are unclear of what that is. Others give into pure science and what can be proven, retreating to the notion that we are simply alive, and then we die. Nothing more.

Figuring this out, finding the answer for myself was complicated. I would think, *If there is a God, a loving God, why would there be so much pain in the world? Why would I work so hard and then be out of a job for no fault of my own?*

Well, I never really found an answer. I guess that is why it's called a mystery of faith, but what I did find was that I wanted to believe that my life had meaning. That I was here for a reason and that I was part of a bigger plan. Was it God? A higher being? Simply pure energy? Or superconscious thought? Infinite wisdom or clarity of self?

I don't know, but what I do believe is that science and faith can live together hand in hand, that they don't have to be at odds with each other. I think that the Big Bang was how the universe came to be, but I also question, "Who lit the fuse?" I don't know, but I do know that life without hope is no life at all. For a life of meaning and purpose to exist, I believe that we must trust that there is a unique plan for us in service to others and that it had to be created by someone or something that I simply refer to as the master of the universe. I'm not here to tell you what to believe, simply to suggest that there is a power greater than ourselves at work in our lives that is the foundation for living a life of meaning and purpose.

I have experienced this firsthand through young people. One of the saddest thoughts I hear over and over again with this incredible group is a lack of belief in anything more significant than themselves, often leaving them empty and void of hope. I struggle with this to this day, knowing what believing has done for me, yet being careful not to force my beliefs on them out of respect and to encourage them to develop their own conclusions. It has been tough for me, often leaving me in tears to know the secrets found along the road to purpose, yet knowing that allowing them the opportunity to discover their own beliefs is where real ownership occurs.

I do believe that we have a place, a purpose, a reason for being but that we must, as Brian Tracy says, "move our feet." That is, wanting it, praying for it, or simply wishing for it is not enough and is denying our very reason for existence. To expect results without some form of action goes against the laws of the universe. Simply put, you can't have an "effect" without a "cause" to make it real. To expect results without some form of action is to deny the universe itself. If we indeed are in control of our thoughts and actions and if we do genuinely believe that our lives have meaning and purpose and that what we do and who we are matters, then we must "move our feet." We must take action. The master of the universe has given us the skills and talents to be our best selves; it is up to us to make the first move, to want it, to pursue it, and to take others along with us.

I waited a very long time to find this gift, the gift of grace, before I finally listened to my heart and started moving my feet.

It scared the hell out of me. It took personal responsibility and a lot of faith to take the first step. And when I did, oh brother, when I exercised free will to move my feet, I tasted the other side and wanted more. I began to believe that life at full potential was not only possible but a responsibility that requires us all to take our place in the world.

So, what is this word "faith"? One of my favorite definitions is believing it to be even if you can't see it, feel it, smell it, or touch it. Faith, in the traditional sense, is a belief in something higher guiding our life. Faith would say that we believe we are created in the image of our maker and have a purpose to live out a life of meaning. For me, to do that, I need to know who I was at the core, in my heart and head, and what I am here to do.

For me, to indeed have faith in something more significant starts with knowing yourself. Having faith in yourself is faith at a much higher level. What I discovered for myself on the road to purpose was that allowing yourself to know that some things just cannot be explained by science or history or fate. Something like a person suffering from stage four cancer living longer than any doctor thought possible or going into complete remission. Like the job offer that shows up right when you needed it most even though you never applied for it. Faith, believing that things happen for a reason, does not only apply to the good stuff in our life. Faith can also test you when things are not so pleasant, like when you lose a job or a loved one before their time. That too, as hard as it might be at the time, faith would say happened for a reason. What is the growth that might come out of it? What learning is the situation forcing on you? How might that improve your life going forward?

For me, leaving my company was the absolute worst thing that could happen to me. Today, I now know more than ever that it happened for a reason, and that reason was to open my heart and my head to people and opportunities that I had blocked out for so long. To allow myself to be happy, to return to a time when I found great joy in helping others, not to be a prisoner of the almighty dollar or prestige or fame that I found myself chasing most of my life. Sometimes the hardest things, the most painful ones, create the most beautiful outcomes when we approach them through faith. Some call this coincidence, other random occurrences. For me, when they come at precisely the right time and in precisely the correct order when you are not looking for them, I have to think that it is neither random nor a coincidence. I believe that this can only be called grace.

I know you have been there before. That answer to that problem that you have been stewing over that came to you right when you needed it most, in detail. For me now, during my morning priming and meditation, solutions to problems fall like rain by merely knowing they will. It's a gift that I don't always deserve and most often one that cannot be explained but almost always one to be shared with others. What a joy it is receiving a gift you didn't expect and being able to share that with others. When problems become gifts, that's grace.

For me, the trauma of leaving my company became the springboard to start my own company. Never would I have taken that risk had my company kept the brands. Or the fraternity that came back into my life as I became a volunteer, 30 years after I had left it, at precisely the right time as I was leaving my company and the team I loved? Together, it allowed me the flexibility to help people have better lives. Also, replacing the often competitive, passive-aggressive, high-stress, and contentious beer and spirits marketing jobs that I thought at the time were the best jobs in the world? I am humbled by it, and you know those voices, they are always telling us we don't deserve it. I am inspired by those it brings into my life and the battles they are fighting, often making mine look like a drop of water in a roaring sea. I have found that it is this precious gift of grace that often brings me to tears, to my knees, wondering, *why me?* Why does this flawed, less-than-perfect man even exist in the universe, let alone benefit from it?

What I believe down deep is that our lives are happening for us, that they happen for a reason, and there's a road map to a grander plan. The clues that provide us the opportunity to find our purpose. When we are doing what we were born to do in service to others is when all the pieces fall in place. While we can move forward through sheer will and determination, when it's not in service to your purpose, it becomes exhausting, like pushing a rock uphill.

What I found at this point in the trip were the beginning phases of clarity, clarity of purpose, and I haven't looked back since. The road to purpose showed me that our lives are resilient. We can do way more, be way more, have way more than our brains want us to. The secret is pushing yourself beyond average, safe, and what you know. Learning only occurs outside your comfort zone.

Growth Through Pain and Relationships

I would continue to connect with old friends along the way who followed their dreams and never gave up. I'm not sure if by design or random acts, but those who I reconnected with all had a similar path they followed: normalcy, pain, resilience, rebirth. Their stories come to life in the journal posts that I would write throughout the trip, but one consistent thing was the opportunity to experience their lives as they were because of the unplanned nature of the journey. No one knew I was stopping in before the trip, so I got to experience their authentic lives full of struggle, kid's sports, work, politics, celebration, and all the joy and challenges that come with it. I asked myself, *Was that the road I was on? Were their lives an example of living my own, accepting my own, and being grateful for the experiences I had instead of killing myself for the life I was living for others?* The answers to these questions and many more would follow along the road to purpose.

I would be tempted one last time by a brewery stop. I hurried through because it was there, no longer because I was there. I would, however, make a couple of quick stops to visit friends who had impacted my work life, made me look good, and, more importantly, made me think differently about human emotion and how to connect it to a brand. I would later learn that the brand I had always been building was my own. They would be those people who no matter what followed their dreams and made it work for themselves, with all the pain and suffering that would usually follow, inside their minds.

I don't know if it's me and my battle with anxiety and depression or it's the intelligent, creative people who I have been so fortunate to call friends, but I find we share similar thoughts. I have found that it is often the people with exceptional brains who suffer silently despite the success they have throughout their lives. They are the people who change things, who move the human race forward.

Often, the people we study in history fall into this category: Albert Einstein, Hemingway, Mozart, Howard Hughes, and Abraham Lincoln, all household names today, prisoners of their minds in their time. People who embraced their experiences, wrapped their minds around them, and focused on doing great things in the world—people like my friend Eric. In his relatively short lifetime, he had lived across the country, been a baseball player, a comedian, a creative director in a world-renowned advertising agency, and now, an agency owner himself. He had this way about him that connected with people and experiences beyond his years. He would make you better by merely listening to his words.

Returning to the road to purpose:

Texas Hill Country would find me holding on to the past but not as tightly as before, what I knew best. I'm starting to understand that true happiness comes not through "things" but experiences. True happiness is merely doing the things you enjoy with the people you enjoy. It's the memories that form that is the real currency of life.

This part of the trip found me doing that with one of the most creative minds I know, a pure genius when it comes to an understanding of the emotional connection of people to products. Eric taught me that the "thing" is simply the tool that binds us, that it's the emotional connection we have with each other that makes us truly happy.

Like so many of us who deal with an often overactive, sometimes relentless, and "exceptional" mind, this insight into the human condition can come with dark and stormy thoughts, tormenting us, keeping us from seeing the real joy in those relationships. Thoughts that when "managed" can help us experience the world in a much deeper way.

A short lesson in Craft Brewers, Micro Distillers, 95 mph speed limits, and lunch with my most creative friend in Austin all make for an excellent day. Lovin' me some TX! Texas Hill Country, TX

Pain can also come in many ways, from incredibly evil acts that human beings do to each other, some without warning that shake the very ground beneath us. Some that move an entire nation to tears. I often wonder why bad things happen to good people. It has caused me to question faith in the past, especially before the road to purpose. What I see now that I didn't understand then is that from "out of the ashes" often comes new growth. That the pain brings hope, and hope brings possibilities. Possibilities, in turn, become purpose and living our intended life. The road to purpose made this very real for me early on in the trip. It was Oklahoma City and the sight of the most horrid act of domestic terrorism ever experienced in our country.

Returning to the road to purpose:

Found myself face-to-face with evil when it landed me in Oklahoma City at the Murrah Federal Building. As I approached the fence around these hallowed grounds, my eyes became fixated on a small, weathered, torn, tattered, faded, once-stuffed teddy bear tied to the chain-link fence. Tears immediately filled my eyes and began rushing uncontrollably down my face. Not a regular thing for me at the time; after all, I didn't know these people. What became readily apparent was that people could do horrible, horrible things to each other. Oklahoma City was the very place where evil, the very devil himself, killed 168 men, women, and children and injured 680 more just as they were starting their day, April 19, 1995... 9:02 a.m.

What I also learned that day was that people, ordinary everyday people with challenges of their own, would step up and provide unconditional and heroic help to others in their time of need. Over the past three years, I have seen this happen again and again. It continues to bring me to tears knowing that regular people living ordinary lives can put everything else aside, including their safety, to come to the aid of strangers, to be true heroes. That somewhere in the darkness, good shines through, that love always triumphs over evil.

The thought of both pure evil and unspeakable grace co-occurring both breaks and inspires the heart. What I know now was that those tears, genuine at the time, might have just been the beginning, the pain that often comes as one begins to transition from past and often empty life to a new and fulfilling one. Like the caterpillar becoming a butterfly, just maybe this was a hint of the years to come and what I would do with the rest of my life: help people in their time of need. Just maybe.

No words today. Oklahoma City Memorial, OK City, OK

With that memory deep in my heart, I would head west. It was approaching Holy Week, and my timing would have me back close to family around the Easter holiday. I had not seen my aunt and godmother in a very long time, and I was so glad it worked out for me to be in Arizona around that time. I would see the sign for old Route 66 and take it for no other reason than the fact it was there. Route 66 had been a thing of the past, a relic of a simpler time. What I would find was an unusual combination of people and roadside attractions that people would visit on long cross-country car trips long before air travel and modern interstate highways existed.

How far I had come in a few short weeks. The anger and blame had pretty much subsided; I was starting to think about what would fill the void. One thing I did learn was that the pain was gone. It wasn't fulfillment that filled the void but pure emptiness. Now that sounds horrible, but I now know that we must first get rid of our past baggage to make room for a new life. While it was scary at the time, disappointing really, it had to happen to open my heart to what was to come. When you get rid of the pain and find emptiness from life's major transitions like breaking up with a girlfriend, getting a divorce, not getting into the school you wanted, or losing your job, hold on. It's part of the process, and what comes next is well worth your trip through emptiness.

Route 66 was a timely and entertaining analogy to bring this uncertain time to life. It would prove to be full of humor, both experiential and self-deprecating, as I took in the seemingly lighthearted, faded, and weathered attractions that littered the roadsides. It was like one day they were "must-see" places, then suddenly, they weren't. Many looked as if people had simply walked away and left them as they were. One such place was a Stonehenge-like attraction made entirely out of old Cadillacs painted psychedelic colors inverted on end that someone had built out in a farmer's field. *Who would do that*? I thought as I chuckled to myself. A whole new way of looking at Cadillacs was not that different than the way I was looking at myself. It was old Route 66 that showed me that I was now open to pretty much anything. I didn't know it then, but I do now that we first must empty the old to make room for the new, and that was what I was doing between Oklahoma and Arizona.

Returning to the road to purpose:

It became clear to me that we should experience life for no other reason than for the experience. The road to purpose found me rising early as the sun was coming up and my cousins were still in bed. I had left my goodbyes the night before with no commitment for the next day, a full heart, and a lot of new perspectives. I asked myself where next, and Albuquerque, NM, popped into my head. I had been there once before on business, so off I went. En route, I started to see some of the old roadside attractions from the Route 66 days, weathered but still standing. Out of nowhere, something popped into my head about aliens and Area 51. Wasn't that somewhere in NM? Midstream, I changed my mind and headed to Roswell.

Lesson learned: It's okay to change your mind, to try new things. Often the road to purpose will point you toward new and mysterious experiences for no other reason than to experience them. Today, I never thought much about this stop but now realize that it was the permission to let go of my past, what I knew, and venture out into the exciting but scary unknown. I now know this was more than just a spontaneous act; it was a turning point, a point that would soon inspire venturing out into significantly a more prominent and more terrifying space, a space that would change my life forever.

...We Americans are a strange lot. Getting my Kicks on Route 66, Tulsa to Roswell, NM

That day, I thought back to just how painful it was when my company decided to sell my brands and how I would see hope for a brighter future come from it. That day, I know that coincidence as grace, an opportunity that made the life I have today possible and one I consider to be the most grateful moment in my life today. Had all the pain of being out of work not occurred, I never would have changed my perspective and never would have experienced the joy I do today. I would have never had a group of young men come into my life who would later be the launchboard for the life of helping people that I live today. Their struggles made mine seem not so big. I would not have had to find empathy when a young man committed suicide a month before I was to become the chapter's counselor. I would not have been there when a second older alumni member would do the same while I was on my trip. I would have never been there for them at precisely the time when life would put into question their idealistic view and excitement for becoming men for the first time, venturing out on their own.

And the kicker, I needed them at precisely the same time they needed me. Together we found meaning and purpose and the knowledge that growth would come from the relationship. That pain has become my sole mission, my purpose, and the driving force of why I do what I do in my personal and professional life today. By touching these lives, I have saved some, but all in some way have saved me from my struggles. Without those struggles, I would never have the unimaginable joy I have today, the life, the path that only became real after the road to purpose.

I had a lot of time between Oklahoma and Arizona to think, to dig deep about how I often saw things in my life as they were, how often I saw reality even though I chose to see it as ideal even when it wasn't. My eyes had been open to a world that had been right out in front of me. I now have clarity and see these times as tests to help build resilience in others that, in turn, creates it in me. I always chalked it up to optimism and have found that while that is perfectly fine, a sense of reality is also important to realize the vision that you set for yourself. You have to know your starting point and be brutally honest with where that is before you can set the path to where you want to go.

The road to purpose had been evaluating how I saw things from this point on. Things like religion, nature, people, what success is, and what the world could be. Knowing what happens to us and what happens for us and knowing the difference between the two. Most important, this notion of being here for a reason and knowing what that means for each of us. This part of the trip and the stops I made along old Route 66 brought that all to light. This part of the journey inspired me to think about how I was judging what was right out in front of me. Why were these attractions there, strange as they were? What was their purpose? Just maybe, they had no purpose at all, or at least no longer had a purpose? Perhaps they were just there, well, because they were there.

The attractions were not the only things that brought up this question of judgment of life in so many ways, often in places that one would never expect. The first was one of the most beautiful places on the trip, White Sands National Park in New Mexico. Imagine, if you will, a desert of pure white sand blown and piled like the beautiful sands of an hourglass set against a bright blue sky. Imagine the sun reflecting in such a way that it was blinding yet warm to the skin. It was peaceful, very spiritual, and it opened my mind to why I was there. It was the first time that the idea of something bigger than myself was driving this trip, and in some way, I knew I was where I was for a reason.

Returning to the road to purpose:

Found myself in one of the most beautiful places on earth, White Sands National Park. Very white, very bright, and if I could imagine heaven, it would look like this. Somewhere between Albuquerque, NM, and Tucson, AZ

After White Sands, I would grab lunch and a beer, make a couple of stops along the road to pick up odds and ends, and head on out to Tucson to spend a couple of days with my aunt. Maureen was more than my aunt; she also held the title of godmother. I was also the oldest child of my generation, providing me the opportunity to be spoiled for almost two years before my brother was born. That time was special to me, a time of curiosity and learning, of being exposed to possibility, and none more than through Maureen.

Maureen is an amazing lady that raised three incredible kids on her own, knows multiple languages, traveled the world, and picked up a Notre Dame law degree along the way. Maureen is a teacher at heart, a person who gains life experiences mostly through building relationships with exciting and unique people and shares those experiences with others. She is an advocate for the underserved and those who society has forgotten. She is a warrior in defense of the environment and makes her voice heard through activism. She is a free spirit and, even in times of great hardship, always finds a way to learn and share that learning with others. She lives an example that values relationships over money as the real currency of life.

Returning to the road to purpose:

The past had left my mind, and I was empty inside, lost, confused, and afraid that the life that I had managed so well was over. Religion was not the answer, even though it was all around me. Spirituality was becoming more real, though. For a person who had struggled all his life with an overactive mind, this was a time of torment. I was now free of the bindings of the past and searching for what would fill the empty void left by it. There could have been no better stop than this one.

Over the next few days, we would explore nature, religion, and how the two come together in Native American traditions. We would celebrate Easter in a Catholic church that accepted everyone for who they were, no matter their past, without judgment and with a friendly, young, Harley-riding priest with long hair. (Not normal for me, but loved the juxtaposition of it all). We would simply hang out and talk about stuff in a way that made me feel free, free to be me, free to be the me I had buried for so long.

What I would learn is that sometimes you just have to "go for it" even when it doesn't make rational sense, even when it doesn't make financial sense, even when all those around you believe it to be the wrong choice. That sometimes just going for it for the sake of following your heart, charting your course, the one that feels right to you, is worth the journey. And whether it turns out the way you planned or not, you always leave with learning. Learning you can use to change the world.

LOVE conquers hate and death. Happy Easter with my Aunt Maureen, Tucson, AZ

Tucson would be the second place that I spent extended time with family along the road to purpose. It wasn't until Tucson and the stops along the way that I would realize that that anger I had experienced so far was what was holding me back. The stops since Tampa had helped empty me of anger, hate, blame, and excuses to make room for the new life I was about to experience. Tucson was that turning point, and my aunt Maureen, as she was so many times when I was a young boy, was that catalyst who started getting me thinking in a different way of what a life of meaning and purpose could become.

Returning to the road to purpose:

Day 2 in Tucson, an essential stop on the journey, found us exploring the incredible place that is Arizona. The desert can seem so inhospitable, dead; nothing grows in it, miserable, hell on earth. Yet when a stream runs through it, seemingly flowing from the rock, life explodes. Flowers, birds, nature in all its forms are as far as the eye can see. I now see this as a metaphor for human existence.

First, our view of the desert, our aspect of life, is all in the way we view it, our perception. If we see it as dead, then dead is what we get. If we look closer and see it as beauty, then beauty is what we get. My learning is that life is not good or bad, not ugly or beautiful, not happy or sad. Life is life, and it's only in how we judge it that brings pain or happiness. That how we view the world and approach it is all in our control. That life is what we make it. That we can have any experience we choose by merely deciding to have it. That, like the desert, our ability to adapt and change is what keeps us happy, which keeps us alive—the idea that our own beliefs are the only things that can limit us.

I also learned that, like the desert, it is essential to have a stream of life, someone who believes in us, who expects the work that leads to lifelong friendships. A person who is willing to cut through rock to help us see potential in ourselves where once only sand existed. Someone who accepts nothing but our best and guides us and shows us that the beauty in our own heart opens up the deserts in our lives and makes way for a life of meaning and purpose.

Yes, at first glance, the desert seems dead and inhospitable. Yet in all its bigness, one finds beauty and new beginnings. In all the silence, one finds peace and a sense of purpose. The many colors of Tucson.

Tucson made clear that the human condition is the celebration of diversity, that everyone has a role to play. My final day in Tucson found me visiting San Xavier del Bac Mission, a place where native American tradition and western religion came together for me. A place that liberated and purified the soul in preparation for the future. It was where I learned that just possibly our spirit, our purpose, lives through our unique diversity, and as the mission chapel, is incomplete, imperfect, unfinished yet beautiful and transforming.

Experiencing Tucson with my teacher showed me that true beauty, like the desert, lies inside each of us, in our unique gifts and through sharing those gifts with the world. That growth only happens when we embrace that diversity. When walking in someone else's shoes helps us walk taller in our own. Where, like the desert, seemingly dead if viewed in parts, comes alive and become breathtakingly beautiful when experienced as a whole. We can only experience the unimaginable beauty of life when we fill the entire canvas with all our colors, victories, broken dreams, strengths, imperfections, confidence, and fears, everything that makes up the mosaic of the human experience.

This part of my trip reinforced what my parents had taught me so many years ago. That everyone, everyone has an important role to play on this earth. Poor, vibrant, black, white, brown, red, every color of the rainbow. Gay, straight, and everything in between. Man, woman, transgender, and all the ways we identify ourselves. Yavapai, Tohono O'odham, Christian, Jew, Muslim, Hindu, believers, and non-believers alike. Every possible version of ourselves as a unique and vital reason to be here. Working in harmony with each other and nature, like the desert, is what creates the masterpiece of our lives and is what truly living is all about.

Returning to the road to purpose:

"And while I stood there I saw more than I can tell, and I understood more than I saw; for I was seeing in a sacred manner the shapes of things in the spirit, and the shapes of all shapes as they must live together like one being."
—Black Elk, Tohono O'odham Nation, San Xavier del Bac Mission, Tucson, AZ

What I learned on this part of the journey is that knowing yourself is about being able to face mountains of challenge and seeing them as speed bumps. You know that you will occasionally slip backward, fail, or face uncertain times, but you also know that you will get past them. Knowing yourself is often all about genuinely believing that things happen for a reason. It's about knowing your trigger points that get in your own way, those things that give you an excuse to give up and give in instead of growing from the pain. It often means knowing the deep, dark secrets that hide inside of all of us that we would like to deny. It's about knowing how they impact us, how they hold us back, and genuinely owning them as part of our unique self.

For me, depression has been that trigger. It has been with me all my life, though not diagnosed until well into adulthood, and you would think by now that I would know how to manage it. For the most part, I do, but occasionally, the reaction to it becomes my most significant burden. My response to depression is often anger, which I struggle to regulate, which means that I, in turn, push people away. This often results in losing some of the people I love most in this world.

Before the road to purpose, I saw them as casualties of my so-called successful life. It, the reaction, not the illness, often took away the very reason to face the mountain itself. I, too, would stumble from time to time and use the disease as an excuse instead of taking responsibility for my feelings and the reaction that sometimes follows.

The reaction usually results from thinking the worst, that the world is out to do me harm. Often, it was nothing more than the way I judged an uncomfortable event then attacking the person I blamed for it.

Since the road to purpose, I continue to struggle with this, and it continues to have similar results, including nearly destroying a friendship that was part of my life since the journey. A painful lesson hard-learned that, by the grace of God and forgiveness, gave me a second chance. It taught me that knowing ourselves is knowing that we are flawed and that doing our best to manage our demons is not always enough.

I will forever be grateful for another problematic and painful lesson on the road to purpose, one this time that saved a friendship and put some boundaries in place that saved me as well. In the end, the universe is unfolding as intended. It never really is as we see it but how we judge it that creates our reaction. While we may not be able to control the situation, we can always control how we respond to it. It is up to us to make it count.

I left early the next morning and headed west. I had traveled across the entire country from the Atlantic to the Pacific, covering thousands of miles and multiple states. The journey zigged and zagged both geographically and through the thoughts that raced through my mind. The one thing that stayed consistent, though, was reconnecting with people just in time to enjoy their real lives and their families with no prior planning. To hear their unique stories and experience their authentic selves helped me create a roadmap for my own life that would follow.

My next stop would be Hollywood, California, to see my cousin Nick. Nick was my aunt Maureen's oldest son and had been by her side through many of the struggles the family faced as any would with a single mom raising three kids. He had grown up much faster than most kids did, often working to help make ends meet, helping out with his younger brother and sister and being a sounding board when he got older.

The family, led by a schoolteacher, didn't have a lot of things, but there was so much love that they would never complain and would remain close to this day. Nick and his brother and sister would become excellent swimmers, and all of them would do well in school, earning scholarships for their efforts and abilities. They would also become a family of activists and fight for the less fortunate in their communities, a place to come together and enjoy each other. Nick, like me, would also have a special relationship with our grandmother, who was often there for both of us as we were growing up. My journal entry tells Nick's story, and we enjoyed our time together, the two oldest sons on our mothers' side of the family, both with independent energy that would prove to work for both of us.

Returning to the road to purpose:

I discovered anything is possible with vision, goals, disciplined focus, and action. The road to purpose found me heading west to the City of Angels, Los Angeles. Next stop cousin Nick's. Nick, my aunt Maureen's oldest son, has had quite the life. He's been a competitive swimmer and a Navy man on the USS America, and he studied political science at Notre Dame and film and theatre at the University of Kansas. Then on to become a restaurant manager, NYC real estate broker, business owner, and now working his way up the hugely competitive ranks as a film producer. Wow!

My stop would find me going directly to the set of the final day of filming a Swedish TV series. How cool was that? That followed by visiting his Hollywood apartment, then on to an after-party. Who gets to see LA this way? A random guy on a random trip at precisely the right time, that's who.

Nick accepted an offer to a prestigious Directors Guild of America program, one of only 12 approved out of thousands of applications. Today he is a Sony DGA Assistant Director. He has produced voice-overs and commercials and has worked on popular shows like The Goldbergs and Speechless, to name just a few. Like so many successful people, Nick started with a dream and pursued it. He had to overcome challenges, and he never gave up. Nick sacrificed and struggled at times financially and otherwise but never lost sight of his goal. Nick had been that way all his life: He decided what he wanted, overcame high barriers, believed, and did it.

What I learned from Nick was that anything is possible if you can think it, believe it, if you are willing to do the work, then you can "achieve it." What I know today is that goals without action are simply fantasies. While the movie business is mostly fantasy, becoming a producer is not. It takes hard work, determination, and a willingness to take risks, fail, and start again, to face sacrifice and perseverance to realize success. While most likely Nick is nowhere near his final stop on his journey, I do not doubt that he can see it in the distance. He has the vision, goals, single focus, and discipline to get there. Nick knows that it takes action to turn those dreams into reality.

A once-in-a-lifetime LA experience with my cousin Nick (he's in the business). Day 1 on set for the final shoot of a new TV series, an after-party with cast and crew, staying in his Hollywood apartment. Powerful creative forces all around me, born to create beauty! Cousin Nick, Hollywood.

Optimism had begun to fill that empty space as I found my way to LA. I had gotten to know myself pretty well by now, what stood in my way, my thoughts and fears, the notion of grace in my life, how I view and judge situations, and what I thought I wanted. I learned that when we have complete clarity in who we are and what we want from our experience, it becomes our reality.

For the young men I worked with, that was a groundbreaking insight that changed their lives. The seasoned professionals finding second careers where they could focus on fulfillment versus power and money would discover that with fulfillment often came power and wealth. We realize that knowing what we want and doing the work to get it is all that stands in between us and success. It all starts with how we define ourselves at our very core, our values.

Three Key Signposts Along the Road to Purpose

1. Start seeing failure as feedback, a true gift to learn from, and move on.
2. Have faith in knowing that life happens for a reason, and learn from it.
3. Almost always, real growth comes through pain. Embrace it; push through it.

Chapter 4

Life's Filters

"Good values are like a magnet—
they attract good people."

—John Wooden

The road to purpose gave me long periods alone and the self-reflection that comes with it. In times like this, you will ask yourself as I did, *What do I stand for? What is my definition of right and wrong? What are the lines I just won't cross at any cost?*

What we stand for is often clouded by other variables that enter our life like, *What does our partner stand for? What does our company stand for? What do the social organizations, schools, or nonprofit groups we volunteer for stand for?* Most of us never think of this, and hardly anyone ever write them down, define them in a way that is meaningful to them and then gauge themselves as to whether or not they are living them. For young people just starting, often what we stand for is what our parents or schools stood for. We are still in the process of forming who we are as individuals. We often find ourselves challenging the values of our parents as we try to establish ourselves as individuals. Most young people I work with have never had to define what they stand for, simply just knowing that they stand for something.

To honestly know yourself, you must know what you stand for. You must know that line that you will never cross no matter what. What determines that line are your values, or what I like to call the filters of your life. They are you, and without them, there is no you. They are those checkpoints that when you cross them, it tears you up inside, makes you feel small, worthless, and ashamed. To honestly know yourself, you must know what you stand for so that you can be your authentic self.

Knowing your values and being clear on what you stand for is what it means to really "know yourself." It is the critical first step in achieving the success and happiness you are looking for in your life. A bright, honest, and precise understanding of who we are, why we exist, how we make decisions, and what others see in us is a must before we can set out to make our mark on the world. Knowing who we are with infinite clarity becomes the starting point for everything else. If you don't know yourself, you will never be yourself and most likely will find it difficult to ever love the person that you have become.

For me, knowing who I am is defined by the filters I use to make decisions, my values. My values are how I live my purpose and, in turn, come to life in what I bring to the world, my talent. We will talk more about purpose and talents a little later in the book, so for now, let's get clear on who we are, starting with values. The values I have chosen for myself guide all my decisions like who I allow in my life, what clients I prefer to work with, where I work, and what causes I support. The values I have chosen for myself have most likely been with me for a very long time but came to the surface along the road to purpose.

For me, they are: 1. curiosity, an insatiable desire to discover who I am, 2. courage, the willingness to be myself for me with no concern for what others think I should be, and 3. compassion, first to love myself so that I can in turn genuinely love all those in my life or yet to be. My journey taught me that defining your values in your own terms, not Webster's, is what is necessary to utilize this vital tool in your life. While these values are mine, I will share with you a little later in this chapter how to define your own. Once you do, things will become more apparent, and you will know your place in the world precisely and later bring that to life through your purpose.

Curiosity

So, if not only the value itself but the definition of that value is essential to guide your life, how have my values, found along the road to purpose, guided my life today? My first value might as well apply to you if you crave understanding yourself during this time of transition. Or possibly you are looking at a second career and what will you need to know to achieve it. If you're a young person trying to figure out what you want to do with your life, maybe the value of curiosity will help you try out new things, experience new groups, or have an opinion on a topic never before had. It worked for me, and now I am living a life distinctly different than the life I thought I would be living at this point.

I have adopted curiosity as my first personal value, and it has been a fantastic filter to regulate my life. Curiosity, to me, is made manifest in the belief that a life well-lived is learning in and of itself and requires an open mind to achieve it. To be curious is to lead a life of creativity, continuous learning, and optimism. Creativity in this context means to inspire creativity in self and others. It's the notion that ordinary people with a passion for finding innovative solutions can achieve extraordinary things through respect for diversity and an ability to capitalize on our collective experiences.

Continuous learning is to search out self-improvement opportunities and to combine that knowledge with experience in pursuit of wisdom, a never-ending commitment to personal development, and an open mind to every life experience. For me, this comes to life in my passion to coach, teach, mentor, and help others, and in doing so, I grow and learn myself.

I believe that curiosity requires infinite and never-ending optimism, a belief that anything is possible, that dreaming big, believing in yourself, and committing to do the work will result in unimagined success. Dreaming BIG is one thing; doing big is another, and that takes planning, the courage to take risks, perseverance, and the discipline to see it through. Curiosity became my number one filter along the road to purpose.

Returning to the road to purpose:

I found that everyone has a story in LA. On day two, cousin Nick went to work, and I decided to get to know the neighborhood on an all-day walk. A complete mosaic of humankind in this very diverse part of the city. The art, interesting homeless people, a family pizza joint where the locals gathered to play cards, all unique in their way, all with a story written on their faces through the lives they lead.

What I learned then was that everyone has a story, and if you take the time to listen, the story comes alive in you that the human condition is nothing more than a collection of stories. Stories, unique in every way that, in some magical way, ties us all together. That when we take time to listen, it allows us to know ourselves better, know our place in the world, and eventually the courage to share our own story.

Getting to know the neighbor and other interesting folks, Hollywood, CA

So, the question I have for you is, what's your story?

Courage

The second value I picked up along the road to purpose was courage. Funny story, during a post-retirement lunch with a co-worker, I was feeling anything but courageous. I had recently left my job, had yet to decide what I was going to do next, and was insecure about my future.

Life transitions often come with an uncomfortable time when you reconnect with the people you worked with. If you are a young person, that might be when you have a bad semester in school and decide to sit out for a while—coming back can be awkward. It's no different when you leave your company after a long career.

For me, that included meeting old friends at a restaurant that employees of my previous company didn't usually frequent. I suspect that was done to not be seen, making it even more awkward. I mean, I only left the company, I'm not dying of some dreaded disease. Nonetheless, you have to have patience with them.

Then the questions start—you know the questions. Questions like: What are you doing now? How has it been since you left? Are you doing okay? And on and on. The real questions they are implying but not asking are, *Aren't you scared to death? What on earth are you going to do now? You're 50+. Isn't it hard finding another job?* The funny thing is that the questions in their heads are most often the same ones you are dealing with inside your own.

With a little compassion for my friend, I thought I would just head the questions off at the pass and get right to the point. When asked how it was going, my response was, "Well, I'm not living my value of courage very well, I'm stepping out into an area I have never been before, and I'm scared to death." She looked me right in the eye and said, "It's not a lack of courage to be scared… courage is being scared and doing it anyway!" Wow, what a thought. I would have many days post-road to purpose that would scare the hell out of me, still do to this day, and with that little piece of insight and the willingness to "do it anyway," things have always worked out for the best.

For those of you in transition, from students to middle-aged employees to business owners, it is courage that will push you through the tough times and courage that helps you see that the grass is greener on the other side. It takes courage to be great. It takes courage to live a prosperous and happy life. It takes courage to realize your dreams. It's easy to be average, mediocre, and safe. Anyone can be secure, and my friend reminded me that at this point on the trip, I gave up that once self-limiting belief of "being average," pushed through the fear, and found an incredible life on the other side of the journey.

You can and will too, but you must first decide to. I would later realize that courage had been a guiding force with me all along. Before leaving my company, it took courage to push the limits in my old position that often put the bean counters on high alert right up to the point of a brand blowing out its financial goals. It took courage to push a century-old company with conservative marketing views to try a new luxury approach versus a traditional brand approach. It took courage to leave an excellent job in a company that I loved for a six-figure pay cut to work on one of America's most iconic brands. It took courage to make the moves that would get me back to that salary I had made at my old company in less than three years. And in the end, it took courage to opt to walk away from the company and venture out on my own at 51 years old. Believe me, I was scared to death—never been that scared before.

Still, I would later realize that it's in action where fear turns to opportunity, where being afraid and doing it anyway sets a pace for a lifetime of success and happiness. The very trip itself without any destination in mind or process for getting there or planned places to sleep was an act of courage, especially for me. That old saying, "If you don't know where you are going, you might just end up somewhere else," is a for-sure recipe for failure. For all of this, courage was the secret ingredient that helped me make that first move and lead to the incredible learning that the first step is always the most difficult and the most important.

So, I ask you, do you have courage buried deep inside you that you need to let out? Are you scared to death and letting that fear hold you back? What do you have to lose? Give it a shot and move past it. That is courage, my friend.

Compassion

My third and most important value would be the one that has guided me all my life: compassion. I had formed a hard shell of protection against emotion, yet the soft underbelly, compassion, remained. Growing up in a family that believed and taught me that it was our responsibility to help others had always been part of my DNA. After the road to purpose, compassion became much more profound for me, vulnerable, almost, in a way.

Giving more than money or time but self, the deepest part of self that in some way allows others to see my flaws and my vulnerabilities, allowed them to be okay with their own. It told them that it was okay to be scared because they had to start a new career all over after 30 years. Or it was okay to be afraid that the perfect job was not going to be there when they graduated. It was "okay to not be okay" in the case of some suffering from depression, anxiety, and in some extreme cases, attempts at suicide.

It's a very different thing when compassion is about sharing your darker side so that others might find light in their struggles. As an adult, compassion more profound and different than my family's had always been with me. My time since the road to purpose has proven to me that genuine compassion, giving for giving's sake, pays back more than I could ever imagine.

In Adam Grant's book, *Give and Take: A Revolutionary Approach to Success*, the author highlights the power of compassion in everyday life. His research looked at people he defined as givers, matchers, and takers. He found that givers, those who provide solutions to others to help them improve their own lives, received more than ten times the value back for their generosity and finished first in measures of success than all others sampled. He found that takers, or those who put their self-interest ahead of others, finished dead last.

I have found that giving helps the giver and the receiver. It provides well-being and life fulfillment. As a side benefit, I have seen it in my own coaching business also as a way to earn a living. I can't think of anything better than helping people for a living, and it all starts with genuine compassion for my clients and others—the compassion that often comes as a result of curiosity and courage and that has provided me with the very recipe for true happiness, happiness found by simply pushing past the pain onto the road to purpose. Opening up to others, genuinely listening and learning from them, is where true human empathy occurs.

So, if values are the filters of our lives and the core ingredient in knowing ourselves, how do we go about defining what they are for us? While our values are different because we all have different experiences in life, the good news is that the process for determining yours is no different than the method for determining mine. Let's first take a look at where we all get our start in building our very own values.

First, values through our experiences provided to us by our parents and other influential people in our life at a young age are our starting point. As an example, the experiences that impacted me came from a traditional Catholic upbringing with values like honesty, integrity, hard work, being self-made, taking care of others, small-town life, personal responsibility, church, and family. These values served me well as a boy and set the stage for a life where anything was possible.

Second, as we grow older, our own experiences and the people we choose to be with begin to mix in with the values given to us by our parents, and we begin to define our own set of values as we enter adult life. For me, this started when I left home for college and joined a fraternity. The words were different but the meaning the same, words like virtue, diligence, and brotherly love aligned well with honesty, hard work, and taking care of others. Later, I would add company values to fill in the gaps in my professional life.

One tip on values and work: Never work for a company that doesn't share your values, no matter how much money or benefits they want to bestow upon you. If your values conflict with the company you work for, you will hate your work and hate working there, and in turn, your performance and reputation will suffer. I was fortunate to have worked for several companies that had strong ties to founding families. When family members were still involved, the values rang true, and the company itself was an extension of them. As they moved on through mergers or new leadership changes, those values usually began to blur, and more economic drivers took over, often at the expense of the employee and customer. When this happens, it is always time to move on.

While we all have values, I have found that not many of us have taken the time to sit down and define what they are and write them down. Writing them down commits us to those values and ensures that you are more likely to live them in your everyday life. When your actions and your values are not aligned, chances are you will not live up to your full potential. At the very least, you will feel uneasy and not like yourself very much. So how do we make that commitment to live our authentic self through our values?

Step 1:   Write down your values.

Step 2:   Define what they mean to you. Use your definition, not necessarily Webster's.

Step 3:   For decisions, ask yourself, "Does this decision align with my values?"

Step 4:   No matter what, if the answer is no, walk away.

Staying true to your values will often be tricky. You may have just left your job and ventured out on your own to start your own business, or maybe you've graduated and will be looking for a company with which to share your talents. You will soon find that not everyone shares your values. You will also most likely be at a place in which earning a living is necessary to pay back those student loans or pay that big mortgage you may have acquired while working.

What I learned is, as much as you want to take that job, if your values are not aligned, you must look for another one. In my business, a big mistake I have seen over and over again is taking clients or customers simply because they have money. Money might make you happy in the short run, especially if you are just starting, but in the long run, it will not overcome conflict in values. Your business will pay back long term if you remain true to your values.

Returning to the road to purpose:

I was at about the halfway point. It would be during my time in Los Angeles, with all the experiences so far with people living their own lives, that I would first start

to think about who I was, what I believed, and what I really stood for, and most importantly, why it mattered. I would later find this to be the seed of purpose that had to elude me all my life. As I was saying goodbye to my cousin and headed out for what would be a couple of weeks of self-awareness, I would start to explore the age-old question of "why." Why it mattered.

It was at this time on the trip that the transition between old and new would become completely clear. It was on this part of the journey where the empty spot inside of me would start to fill again, rebuild, and accelerate. It was on this part of the trip that my values, not my companies, would bear themselves as curiosity, courage, and compassion. Guided by these values, little did I know of the epiphany that would come in the days ahead.

What I learned is that you must first get rid of the old paradigms to make room for what was to come, what had always been buried deep beneath what I had become for others — the real me, not me I thought I should be for everyone else. Like a caterpillar getting ready to become a butterfly, I would soon find the beauty that life would later present to me the experience, the people, and the work that would answer that age-old question for me: "Why?" Why was I here? Why did I let life happen to me? Why was I chosen to do what I do? Why did it matter to the people around me?

My post that the final day would sum it up best and brought it all to life while hanging with my cousin, as authentic a man as one could be. Nick truly knew who he was and what he wanted out of life. Our final night together was seeing a movie in an authentic movie house in Hollywood. My post that day was as authentic as the man I shared the experience with: "Incredible finish for a great couple of days with cousin Nick… Batman vs. Superman in a classic movie theatre where the age-old advertising played on the retro screen "Let's all go to the lobby… let's all go to the lobby and get ourselves a treat." Hollywood, CA

The importance of first knowing yourself became very clear in the first part of the journey when I faced pain, emptied all the noise, and went to work defining the filters that I would use going forward. Will it be easy for you? No. Will it be worth it in the end? Very much yes, especially if you have lost track of yourself over the years. You must know yourself before you can be yourself. You must have a good grip on where you have been and what circumstances and experiences make you, well, you. You must know what gets in your own way, what keeps you from realizing your best self. You must know your triggers and what you are capable of being, doing, and having, and finally, you must know your filters, your values, what you stand for no matter what. Armed with newfound self-awareness, we are now ready to get on to the hard part: being ourselves, our true, authentic selves. What I learned was that authenticity, knowing, and being your authentic self is where success and happiness both come together.

Three Signposts Along the Road to Purpose

1. You are your values—embrace them.
2. Write down and define your values as they relate to you.
3. Use your values as filters to guide your life, and never violate them.

SECTION II

THE COURAGE
TO BE YOURSELF

"To be yourself in a world that is constantly trying to make you something else is the greatest accomplishment."

—Ralph Waldo Emerson

Chapter 5

Pushed To Purpose

"The two most important days in your life are the day you are born and the day you find out why."

—Mark Twain

Joel Osteen, Pastor of Lakewood Church in Houston, Texas, points out that we are often "pushed into purpose" by God when we get too comfortable. I wonder if that has been my story, armed with free will, an insatiable appetite for achievement, and an ego that wouldn't allow for quitting, I often found myself succeeding but exhausted. Looking back, I wonder if that was because I was out of step with what I would soon learn to be my purpose and what I was meant to do with my life on earth.

The next few days on the trip, in some of the most inhospitable deserts between LA and the Grand Canyon, one thing became clear: When you spend a lot of time alone with yourself in a car, you get to know a lot about yourself. You begin to understand how you think, how you feel about thinking, and how you react to things. Not all of what I learned was good, especially at first. Getting to know yourself is not easy for people like me who spend a lot of time thinking about what other people want us to be. We become so fearful of rejection that we become people-pleasers and, at the extreme, co-dependent. In short, we determine our value in how we perceive others' value of us.

When we finally get away from all those who we feel a need to be something other than ourselves for, we experience freedom for the first time. When we can no longer use our busy life, our job, our boss, our teachers, or our friends as an excuse for not being happy, all we have left is ourselves and a lot of time. That can be a scary thing but an essential part of the growth process. When we wrap ourselves up in being whatever it takes for others long enough, we often lose track of who we are for ourselves.

We tell ourselves that we are "doing it for the company" or "doing it for the team," but what we are doing is filling up the time so that we don't have to be alone with our thoughts. Often, it's not because they asked us to be different or even expected us to; it is merely the voices in our head telling us to be something different. When it doesn't work out the way we wanted it to, whether through a breakup or losing the job you love or the one you wanted and didn't get, it leaves a deep hole in our hearts. One that, if left to rot, destroys our very sense of meaning.

I've been there, and the outcome can leave us empty and alone, often angry, depressed, or worse. What I found on the road to purpose was that it all starts with being who we are. It's all up to us to be accountable and do what is authentic to us. We are only responsible for ourselves and no one else. What we believe about ourselves is all that matters. So often, we become who we think we should be for others, and in doing so, we lose complete track of who we are.

Now that we have at least an understanding of ourselves, the next step is to put our newfound knowledge to work, to make it real, actually to start living our authentic lives. I found this to be especially hard for me. Looking back now, I realized that I had spent most of my life living what I thought others wanted me to be. After a lifetime of people-pleasing, it had become a habit, leaving that bad idea engraved deep in my subconscious. Knowing yourself isn't easy, but you must get to that point before you can start to become the person you were meant to be. You must first empty the noise, the anger, and the excuses and swim through the uncharted sea of emptiness that is left. You must then get on to rebuilding your life.

At this point in the trip, I had a new understanding of who I was and who I needed to be. I realized that things would get in the way of me moving forward from time to time, and that's okay. I would have a plan to get around, over, or through them. I had identified what it was that I did best. I was also starting to feel what it was like to have meaning in my life again and a little more courage to be my authentic self.

I was somewhere in the deserts between LA and Arizona when I also began to see that this trip and every part of it was happening for me, not to me. The people, the random nature of the journey, and the time alone with my thoughts all made it clear that the universe was unfolding as intended; I was starting to see the light at the end of the tunnel. I learned that the secret to success was perseverance, pushing forward, never quitting. I realized that happiness is not about things or fame or pleasure or pleasing people but that it was really about being grateful for who we are and the gifts that we have inside of us.

Most of all, I learned that life is not as it is but how we judge it. That often, the circumstance itself is not in our control; instead, it is how we react to it that matters. What if all that had happened at my company—the leaving, the anger, the family and friends who randomly entered my life over the past month—had all been to help me judge the circumstances differently? What if all the pain, sacrifice, and triumph of the people were lessons on life? I'm sure if you asked them, they would say that it was just what life is all about. For me this time, when I needed to be reminded most, it was a signpost for how I was to live my life going forward. I thought to myself, *What if life was happening for me, not to me?*

Armed with my newfound authenticity, the trip had me crossing the desert on my way to Las Vegas. Along the way, I saw a roadside sign advertising a tourist attraction called the "Neon Boneyard" just outside Las Vegas. As a marketer, I was into advertising, and nowhere on earth was there a better example than the city of lights. The graveyard displayed signs from the past that built what we know today as the entertainment capital of the world. The Neon Boneyard was a place where signs would go to die but never deteriorate, now a tourist attraction. For me, it was a place of interest for a guy who had spent his entire career in marketing and advertising.

As I approached Las Vegas and found my way to the ticket window, I found it to be closed for the day. I was a little disappointed but not really. As I pulled out of town, I thought to myself, "not a big deal," and knew at that very moment that my old life was no longer relevant to me. My reaction scared me a bit. A tear rolled down my face as I mourned nearly 30 years of what had been my life while simultaneously feeling a sense of relief set in. I was at peace with my past and ready for what was next.

Returning to the road to purpose:

Somewhere between LA and Las Vegas, it became clear that I was to let go of the past to make room to dream of the future. As I departed LA still holding on slightly to my marketing past, at least the fun part, the creative part, I thought Las Vegas would be an exciting stopover. It didn't happen. As fate would have it, my quest to see the sign graveyard didn't happen.

The Neon Boneyard, as I understand it, is where signs from bygone days of Las Vegas go to die every time a casino is renovated, torn down, or made way for new and different. As a past advertising guy, this attraction was a marketer's dream, a complete tribute to excess and waste. I had to see it! This hot and dry place, signs go to die on the inside, the metal exterior continues, free of rust and decay on the outside. For whatever reason on this day, that attraction upon arrival was closed to the public. Signs that looked great on the outside yet dead on the inside in ways paralleled my life of marketing. On the outside, a world-class marketer with award-winning advertising, on the inside, dead, no meaning or purpose.

Is it possible that this stop was a coincidence or a message from something bigger than myself? Was it time to let go of the life of excess, pleasure, and always looking for that next hit of dopamine that comes with a brand's reaction to a creative message that you played a role in building?

What I know today is that what was happening on the outside was simply a result of what was happening on the inside, something I would later realize had nothing to do with marketing. Today I know that who you are on the inside becomes your reality on the outside. You simply have to get rid of the past, past thoughts, and sometimes past people to make room for new and better things. What's left plus what's new leads to an incredible opportunity for growth.

The Simon and Garfunkel song "sound of silence" came back to me like it was yesterday, that day in junior high chorus where we performed the song as part of the class project. Some of those words seemed fitting... "as

> *we bowed and prayed to the neon god we made. That echoed in the sound of silence," danced in my head as I drove through Las Vegas, headed to Hoover Dam.*

The next location would prove to be a testament to human potential when you believe that you can change things. My journey would begin to evolve in ways that I would have never experienced without the pain that came with transition and the remarkable discovery that I found on the other side of my comfort zone.

I had never been to the Hoover Dam, like so many places located in what I had called the "flyover states." I hardly noticed the land as I moved between areas of commerce on the east and west coasts. I never had taken the time to experience the newfound beauty of this part of the country before. I thought to myself, what the hell? I had extra time (as if time even mattered on this trip), and it was there. No reason, just there, and I was curious. The Hoover Dam impacted me, as it had so many before, and set the stage for what would be the building of the life to come. What I wrote in my journal that day was a premonition of what was to follow in my own life, an analogy of what was to come, the idea of what was possible.

Returning to the road to purpose:

> *The Hoover Dam, this amazing symbol of human ingenuity and the capacity of man to change things, to impact the world in enormous ways, was impressive. Its massive size was erected during the Great Depression to put people back to work, workers who were suffering*

yet found inside themselves the capacity to do great things on projects that served humankind. Was serving humanity my destination as well? Despite the disappointment of the past, was I meant to do great things, great things for humanity?

Once I reached Hoover Dam, a single question haunted my thoughts: "If we can tame the Colorado River and provide clean energy for millions, surely, we can find a sustainable, clean, and safe way to power the planet!" Hoover Dam, Black Canyon, AZ/NV

That vision would stick with me for the remainder of the trip and, to this day, I am still striving to do just that with the people I have been so fortunate to share my time with. The first notion of helping others do great things became my daily obsession. The question: *How would I do that?*

Well, not so fast. Inspired by what I had just seen, I couldn't wait to get on with my journey. As I left the Hoover Dam, I found myself in miles and miles of desert with no sign of life anywhere. About a mile out of town, I was presented with another test, a little speed bump that had my heart pumping as it had never beaten before. I forgot to take care of myself, my car, more like, and learned a precious lesson of what it's like to be running out of gas with only sand and cactus as far as the eye can see. Well, the universe came through again, and I made it, literally coasting into the only gas station in 100 miles on fumes. Lesson learned and a quirky reminder that if my future included great things, I would need a plan.

Returning to the road to purpose:

> *Found me learning a valuable lesson: Planning Greg would get gas at 1/4 tank, spontaneous Greg discovered that there was one gas station between Hoover Dam and Kingman, AZ, offering burgers, machine gun shooting, photo op cutouts, and $4.99/gal gas. The name of the station? "U.R.A.N.U.S." No kidding!*

I guess you had to be there. Why this was significant was because just as I had begun to get back to my usual forward-looking self, I hit a speed bump. Not a big one, but believe me, to this guy who was used to pretty much everything being in place, the chance of running out of gas in the desert would have not only been stupid but dangerous. It reminded me that being spontaneous does not always mean being reckless. As things turned out, I can look back now and laugh, but at the time, it was far from funny.

With a tank full of liquid gold, I once again headed east with the intent of getting to Kingman, Arizona, for the night. I had googled a couple of hotels and realized the area was crawling with them, allowing me to walk up and get a room at the last minute. Kingman was the place where I would head north to visit an old fraternity brother in Idaho. What would transpire at the end of the day was nothing short of a miracle. What I would see would change the way I look at things forever.

If you haven't made the trip by car from the Grand Canyon straight north through Utah, you haven't seen beauty. Incredible rock sculptures millions of years old. An infinite and changing pallet of color as the sun moves from dawn to dusk and open spaces as far as the eye can see. Utah is a state that has true beauty that must be experienced in person.

While my corporate life had given me many experiences that most people never get to see, none compared to the beauty of the Grand Canyon, a place I would have never set out for as a destination, an opportunity I would have never given myself. This one, though, reached out and grabbed me as if the master of the universe was saying, *Look what I can do. You, you're small, very small in comparison, yet you are an even bigger masterpiece.*

Leaving the Grand Canyon, I knew that I was ready to fill my vessel and live the life that would follow. That place? Grand Canyon National Park, South Rim.

Returning to the road to purpose:

Leaving my past baggage scattered along the road, I was now empty of the past and opened, ready to fill myself back up with future hopes and dreams, friendships, challenges, and meaning of purpose.

I had spent most of the day driving in the desert and found my way to Grand Canyon National Park. The sun was setting, and having never seen it, I thought, what the hell, I'll stop and see this giant "empty" hole in the ground, and check the box. What I found was pure beauty like I had never experienced—every color of the rainbow and many, many more. Trees and flowers were growing out of the rock, and vastness, massiveness in every way. A giant hole, yes, but a vessel that was not empty at all but one full of beauty like I had never seen before.

Late in the day, I was mostly alone with myself and the incredible peace that comes with being in the presence of nature and realizing that I was nothing but a grain of sand, a droplet of water in this thing we call life. I soon realized that grain of sand or that droplet of water through years of wind and rain had carved this beautiful masterpiece.

Like the Grand Canyon, we, too, have the power to create beauty in the world. While it takes pain, suffering, and determination, anything is possible with love, intention, and perseverance. When people's dreams are important to us, we stop and see the beauty in them and realize their impact on shaping the masterpiece that is our life. We cherish and hold dear the many grains of sand and droplets that fill up the vessel that is our heart, the very source of living a life of meaning and purpose.

7 days, no way! Seven million years to create this masterpiece and still working on it. One of the most beautiful and awe-inspiring places on earth, Grand Canyon National Park, South Rim, AZ

The remainder of the trip and the amazing grace and mercy that would come with it would fill my vessel, fill my life with meaning and purpose. That night, I would never make it to Kingman and chose instead to sleep in my car on the south edge of this masterpiece. The sun had set, and with the sun setting, a sense of peace like I hadn't experienced in a very long time overcame my thoughts. It crossed my mind that if I had stopped for the sign graveyard in Vegas, I would not have been where I was as the sun set on the Grand Canyon.

Life was happening to me. I was where I was supposed to be, and I could feel it in every part of my being. It was as if all the stress had left my body. The tears, happy tears, began to fall again as they often do when I am overwhelmed with awe and wonder. The anger and depression were now replaced with hope and dreams. In a place of unimaginable beauty, gratitude filled the spot that was once empty. I, for the first time, felt like God was in the car with me. I know now that actually, she was there all along. I had let my self-pity keep me from experiencing his presence for way too long.

Earlier in this book, I had introduced you to Dr. Martin Seligman. His research and findings around the power of positive psychology have opened my eyes to the strength we human beings have already inside each of us. I have become a disciple of his teaching. He often talks about the need to fill the empty space left inside after we overcome depression with fulfillment. I could not help but see the analogy in what I was experiencing during my time at the Grand Canyon. If we see our lives as empty, we will feel empty. In reality, our lives are full. Like the Grand Canyon that is full of beauty, we have a life that is full of people who love us, experiences that help us grow and find meaning and purpose.

Grand Canyon National Park, this most beautiful of places and all that had transpired before would never have been held in my heart had all the pain not guided me to make a change. My vision of the future would start here. My past was now in the past, and I was ready to embrace the future. I began to understand why I was here and why it mattered. From this place forward, I would learn what it meant to flourish for the first time in my adult life. That notion would continue to build as the canyon of my own life began to fill with meaning and purpose.

Returning to the road to purpose:

After experiencing a night of some of the best sleep I had had in months, in my car, by the way, I awoke with the sun coming up on the south rim of the Grand Canyon. Majesty, beauty beyond words, and with a sense of peace and self-actualization in my heart, I headed north through Utah.

Utah, like so many other mountain states, was what we referred to as a "flyover state." A part of the country that was barren, with no business or professional value, only places that took up time, areas you had to cross to get to the economic kingdoms of California, the west coast, and beyond. What I discovered was beauty like I had never experienced before, a beauty that had always been there. I had been all over the world, and no place was more beautiful than Utah. This was land I had judged as a barrier, only in my way to where I wanted to go, without genuinely knowing its glory. I don't know whether it was the incredible peace of mind, a genuinely self-actualizing experience, or being in the car by myself for 12 hours (or was I?).

I started to wonder about my life up to this point. How many experiences had I approached as "flyover states"? How many people, "flyover people" had I judged and missed the chance to know on a deeper level? How many dreams, "flyover dreams," had I not allowed myself to have? How much potential missed because of fear, comfort, attitude? How many things, people, experiences had I judged and "flew over" without genuinely knowing... without genuinely knowing myself?

What I learned on this part of the trip was that in the hectic pace of life, we often make excuses, blame others, and hold onto the past. And in so doing, we often miss the beauty that is all around us. When we focus on things, power, money, regrets, judgments, or something we think we want (or should want), we ignore what the universe is placing right in front of us. We genuinely miss opportunities meant as signposts that guide us toward a life of meaning and purpose.

Was I alone in my car for 12 hours in the deserts of Utah? Meaning and purpose, the very master of the universe, was riding along in my passenger seat and most likely had been there throughout my entire life. I now had the tools, the insights to build an incredible life. Incredible natural sculptures that words or photographs could never explain. I will return here one day. Journey through Utah on my way to Idaho.

Pain to Purpose

I am convinced that to be yourself indeed, you must first know why you exist, your purpose. Knowing your purpose, your personal why, your reason for getting up in the morning and the last thing you think about at night, is critical. It guides the direction of a successful and fulfilling life. Before the road to purpose, I had no idea what purpose was, setting it aside as possibly a biblical thing or the latest self-help buzzword. What I know now is that nothing else matters without a clear understanding of why you do what you do, and even more important, that you can articulate it, write it down, ponder it, make adjustments, and finally live it the rest of your life. Without this, nothing else really matters. It's at the core of bringing your values to life. Simply put, it is you at your heart. Without it, we float aimlessly from place to place like a speck of dust in the wind. Armed with purpose, we are a mighty mountain that approaches life with intent and enthusiasm.

So, what does it mean to have a purpose? To me, purpose is that one thing that we and only we can do in service to others. I believe that we all have our own unique and different purpose, that like fingerprints, each is unique to only us. It's that one thing we do that impacts other people. It's why we are on the planet and our contribution to society. Mark Twain said it best when he said, "The two most important days of your life are the day you were born and the day you find out why." Purpose is our why.

As the title of this book reveals, by far the most important lesson I learned was the power of purpose. It's finding that one thing inside of you that you and only you can give to the world. Purpose is the driver that makes you feel like you can't wait to do what you do every day when your feet first hit the floor. Purpose is what gives your life meaning. Without purpose, nothing else really matters. Without purpose, we don't matter.

The road to purpose brought this to life in so many ways, often in places that one would never expect. To me, purpose is that gift given to each of us from the master of the universe. Purpose was the building block of getting to know and like myself. The trip would prove to me that no matter how much I tried to run from it, no matter my faith or lack thereof, whether I believe or not, the question that always rings true for me was, "What is my reason to be, and why am I here?" This eternal question has been at the foundation of all great things and those not-so-great things, good and evil, love and hate, science and religion, all put in place to answer this one question.

I talked earlier about my struggle with organized religion and how I often saw it as a source of the problems associated with answering this eternal question. What it is, without question, though, is that life has "meaning and purpose." We are here for a reason. Everything happens for a reason. This thought and finding that answer was first revealed to me in New Mexico and confirmed at the Grand Canyon, and it would later become intensely clear. Why I was here and why it mattered began to grow at this point on the trip.

Returning to the road to purpose:

Two weeks ago, I thought God was speaking to me through Garth Brooks songs. Today, I'm convinced she was in the car with me! That in the most beautiful land on earth, the Apache Nation, where the first hint of my purpose revealed itself. I do believe, now more than ever, that we all have a unique purpose in life given to us by our creator. That while we all have our purpose, it is up to us to discover it and live it.

Discovery and growth always seem to come through pain for me. The trip itself was exactly the journey that I needed to move to the next level in my life. A journey of grief and self-reflection around the question of who I was and why I mattered. The gift, as it turned out, came wrapped up in the suffering that would follow. The gift was the answer to that question of purpose.

Finding our purpose can be as simple as asking ourselves, "Why do I exist, and why do others care?" Purpose is what motivates us, it's the talents we bring to the world, and it's those things that, no matter how difficult they become, never feel like work when we are doing them. What is that thing that when we are doing it, we are so good at it, we love it so much that we lose track of time? What talent do we bring to the world in service to others? To understand this, we must first understand what it is that we do that brings value to others.

Motivation and Flow

Let's take a look at these two signposts and what we mean by motivation and flow. The American Psychological Association defines motivation as stimuli that induce behavior to take action. They go on to say that, *"In the absence of motivation, ability or potential cannot be transformed."* Motivations have been with us for centuries. Ancient Greeks used the word "Arete" to define this notion of motivation, which is defined by Wikipedia:

> *Arete* (Greek: ἀρετή), in its basic sense, means "excellence of any kind." The term may also mean "moral virtue." In its earliest appearance in Greek, this notion of excellence bound up with the idea of the fulfillment of purpose or function: the act of living up to one's full potential.

Both definitions define that one must live up to their full potential to fulfill their purpose. We must first maximize our talents in service to others to realize our full potential to impact the world around us.

I have found that motivation appears in two forms: the fear of loss and the pleasure of gain. The proverbial carrot and the stick, if you will. What I learned most about myself was that the fear of losing everything was paralyzing, yet a motivation that left one with no other option but to move forward. My time out of work, the situation itself, was not the motivator. Instead, it was the way I saw my life, the way I judged myself that scared the hell out of me. Even though I had lived a practical life and managed money well, that time had me fearing the extremes of losing everything, my family, my home, and everything else I had worked so hard for all my life. Fear of loss of any kind—livelihood, status, acceptance—can push you forward or paralyze you in your tracks. When we focus on the fear of loss, we seldom see the opportunity for gain even when it is all around us. Motivation driven by fear is a powerful thing, often twice as powerful as motivation from gain.

Motivation from gain can also be a powerful thing. The desire for recognition or becoming a leader in your field can be incredibly intoxicating. The road to purpose showed me that motivation driven by pleasure could be powerful; money, love, sex, things, and achievement have inspired many to reach incredible success. Motivation created through pleasure stimulates neurotransmitters like dopamine, serotonin, oxytocin, and other "feel-good" brain chemicals, powerful but usually short-lived experiences.

Real and long-lasting motivation comes from doing those things that you enjoy. That one thing that you do everyday that adds value, that you are known for, that carries the world forward. It could be a career, a task, hobby, or activity that when you do it, you lose track of time. You are so focused on that activity that incredible results seem to come with minimal effort or time. This state of mind is often known as "flow" or "being in the zone." Dr. Martin Seligman in his book, *Learned Optimism*, suggests that true happiness is going beyond pleasure and having the courage to do that thing that puts you into states of flow. That lasting happiness comes in sharing your talent in service to others. To me, that is motivation at its core, when contributing to the greater good is stronger than short-term pleasure. Using your talents in service to others is where your meaning and purpose lies, the secret to true happiness.

Dr. Seligman's theory seems like common sense, but in my time since the road to purpose, I have seen very high performers, students, and professionals alike that achieve all kinds of great things yet are empty inside. Their motivation is in what they believe they should be doing and not what they were born to do. I've worked with young people who chased degrees in areas like engineering, computer science, medicine, law, and other careers based on the perception of how much money they will make or what would make their parents proud. I've met many who failed. I've also met many who pursued passions like art, music, psychology—embracing their purpose, their contributions to the world—who went on to change the world. They were motivated by their action, often resulting in a career path that rocketed them to the top of their field.

I chased that dream of "world's greatest marketer" most of my life. I had the opportunity to create incredible products that went on to become billion-dollar brands. I had the opportunity to develop advertising that tested in the top five percent of all ads produced worldwide. I've turned brands around, delivering revenue that even the finance people didn't believe was possible. All of that and empty inside, unfulfilled. Can any of you relate to this?

On paper success, inside empty. Looking back, the anger, depression, excessive eating, drinking, or any number of self-destructive behaviors usually followed, but you know, I was doing it in the name of the company—well, that's what I told myself, anyway. Let me just tell you, that life was never a winning game plan. No one can sustain it and, eventually, your brain and then your body will give in. The road to purpose showed me that it was never the marketing but the incredible teams of people with limited resources and experience working on brands that impacted the company's bottom line. It was never about the success of the brands that put me into states of flow but coaching the team to do great things that was the driving force. It wasn't until I left my career that I realized this—what a gift.

Utilizing your talent, doing that one thing that you lose time doing, creates motivation to do something even bigger like serving people. It's purpose that, in turn, leads to a life of fulfillment, a life where all else falls into place. Motivation is what keeps you focused. Motivation is what keeps you moving forward. Motivation and the discipline to take action is what I know now separates the successful, the happy, from the average. In the end, motivation is the thing that gets us to do something when we no longer find excuses not to do it. Where completing the task becomes more meaningful than not, when meaning and purpose come alive. When you maximize your talent to the point of flow, you can achieve pretty much anything you desire—most of all, lasting happiness.

Returning to the road to purpose:

With 12 hours of Utah and all its glory now behind me and a heart full of "meaning and purpose," I headed north to Boise, Idaho, to visit a longtime friend and fraternity brother, Shannon, and his family. Shannon was one of those longtime friends that you have that no matter where you are, you always know he will be there for you if you need him. Years may pass, and life may get in the way, but you always know that when you

are togetherr, within minutes, it feels like you were never apart.

This stop, more than three days, reminded me that even though the trip so far had been about emptying the noise of my life, some things stay like the few but special people who are with you even when you are apart. As you empty your heart of the past, that the people appointed by the universe to guide you seem to hold on, people like Shannon and my fraternity brothers. That just maybe, they were there all along to encourage me, push me to actually step out into the unknown, to help me face my fears and find the unimaginable courage that often comes with taking the road less traveled, the way to a life of meaning and purpose. Later, that learning would prove to be true of my closest fraternity brothers, family, mentors, and friends of the past that stood by me through good and bad times and a whole new group of young brothers and friends that would later join the journey in the years that followed. A gift I now know as grace.

Shannon, I, and three other brothers spent our final collegiate year together in a small apartment. Now, 30+ years later, we still get together on occasion and pick right up where we left off. Wouldn't have missed an ID stop for the world... friends and brothers for life! Shannon and Shelly, Boise, ID

Returning to the road to purpose:

Day 2: A Lake, a cabin, mountains, brewpubs on every corner. Hospitality on steroids and a town and people like no other, Shelly and Shannon's little piece of heaven, McCall, ID

Day 3: The road to heaven and back included a stop at Shannon and Shelly's favorite (now mine too) biker bar (they are both Harley riders), "The Dirty Shame Cafe" where the quote from the stage said it all: "My truck broke down in 1970, and I never left…" I play for alcohol! Somewhere in God's country, ID

My time in Idaho was an affirmation that I had all I needed inside of me to find happiness. The time was spent simply enjoying time with friends who didn't judge me, who simply wanted to sit down, have a beer, and share our lives since we last were together. It was relaxing and reassuring to know that I could simply be myself, no layers or self-marketing, just be me, and that was okay. Idaho was about the beauty of the place, the mountains, the roaring rivers, and the wide-open spaces, but more so about the beauty of the people that made me feel okay to be myself. You know the feeling when you can take off your mask and just be you? That is what Idaho gave back to me, the permission to be my authentic self.

After three amazing days in Idaho, I headed east, well southeast, through parts of Wyoming and back through Utah to get one last glimpse of heaven and the birthplace of my very own "meaning and purpose." For me, meaning and purpose is a birthright. It is the unique qualities that each of us has, that only we have, that make us relevant and valuable to others. It is who we are in our hearts and the contribution we were born to make to others. I believe that it is given to us by the master of the universe, by our creator at birth. Meaning and purpose is our assignment for what we are to do with our time here on earth. Here's the catch: It's entirely up to us to discover it for ourselves, and when we do, hold on; the most beautiful life, the most happiness, fulfillment, and bliss awaits us at overwhelming levels.

Armed now with a quick fill heart, I was anxious to decide just exactly what I was to do with my new life. And what better place to figure that out than Colorado, my happy place? My family hangout. The place where I would go when life's troubles were at my doorstep. Troubles like my first engagement, then back again when it was over. A place I would celebrate with friends, grow closer to family, and learn to ski. A place that symbolized the result of hard work by my family and the place of unimaginable beauty to take a break from it all. The place where I would later sit down with the most influential people in my life to help me leap into business ownership. The very place where mountains once represented an insurmountable obstacle on my way to happiness, now seen as an opportunity to conquer. The place where it became clear what I was to do next in service to my newfound purpose to simply *believe, to aspire to inspire greatness in others so that they can positively impact the world.* The rest of the trip would be exactly that: finding the "how" to do that and "what" it would look like.

Returning to the road to purpose:

One month and 7,000 miles behind us, an office day for me and spa day for my horse (actually 700 of them). You know you're on a road trip when you have to stop for an oil change and a bath along the way! Mountain Chevrolet, Glenwood Springs, CO

For those of you who are familiar with the area between the Utah–Colorado border and Vail, Colorado, you know that it's a winding interstate flanked by the Rocky Mountains range on either side. It's a long, narrow canyon lined with small towns and open spaces and the most beautiful vistas on earth. The first stop after getting my car serviced landed me in Vail for a few days to take care of some business that had popped up and, quite frankly, to take a break from the road in one of the most inspiring places on earth. Amongst the incredible massiveness of the Rocky Mountain range, one feels quite small, and with that smallness, the weight of the world is lifted from your shoulders. In some strange way, you feel like you belong, that you are where you should be. In being one with nature, you feel free of the stress of everyday life. For me, it was an opportunity to open my mind up to the possibility of using my newfound "purpose" to impact the world in a positive way.

It was on this day that the "what" to my purpose rained upon me with clarity like never before. Part of my to-do list for the day included following up on several business ownership opportunities that I had started to explore before the trip. They ranged from beverage distribution to pet stores, from brewpubs to cleaning companies, from property management companies to real estate deals. I did not want to be bothered by reality while on my journey, so I would ignore the calls that came in along the way. On this day, I would return those calls. While some excited me more than others, none hit the spot. I began to ask myself, *Why don't you just double down on your philanthropy work with the mentoring organizations and other volunteer positions and boards?* Could I spend the rest of my life as a "super volunteer" with the organizations I love? I had seen firsthand how they improve the lives of young people in exponential ways, these incredible organizations that I support to this day.

Hiding Out in the Open

Each night, my wife Donna and I talked by phone, and the topic of business ownership came up. I expressed no real excitement about my conversations earlier that day, and she responded with the question that has stuck with me ever since: "I don't know why you don't do that business coaching thing." My response, well, "I'm a marketer, why do you think I'm even qualified to own a coaching company?" Her response, "You have been coaching all your life!" "What do you mean?" I replied. She answered, "Big Brothers Big Sisters? Mentoring at UofL? Fraternity mentoring? At work, all you ever talked about was the fabulous teams of talented young people that did incredible things. It was always about them, the people you led who created great marketing, not the marketing itself!"

As we hung up the phone, I dismissed her comments and went to bed. Somewhere in the night, I awoke to the idea of mentoring for a living and couldn't get my wife's words out of my head. What if I had been living my purpose all my life but until this very moment hadn't realize it? What if the noise of life had kept me from what was hiding right out in the open? What if?

What a thought, one powerful question, one right in front of me that I could not see for myself, an idea that I would later realize as a way to live out my purpose in an exponential way. This time, the master of the universe was planting seeds through my wife. Oh, and the company? One with a partner and now good friend and a set of guiding principles that aligned perfectly with my own. One that I would later know as the "pebble on the pond" and one that would play a significant role in the course of life that followed.

Returning to the road to purpose:

Found myself celebrating the halfway mark with some old friends and creative team from my past: Jack (Daniels), Jim (Beam), and Bud (Weiser). As I looked out at the vista from my back porch, I couldn't help but recall a few lines from the poet Aztlanquill that went something like this: "When the pressures of the world are way too much to bear, I climb to the summit, up the side of the mountain I trod, I raise my hand to the skies and touch the face of God." Final night, Vail, CO

With my business catch-up behind me, I headed east to Denver. The two-hour drive down the mountain had me thinking that the road to purpose had produced several casualties along the way. Gone were things like self-limiting beliefs, insecurities, fear, and all those people who came into my life for a reason at the time but didn't stick around when my life changed. We all have these people, and they play an essential role yet move on to make room for new ones. While this may seem sad, it is as the master of the universe designed it to be and should be celebrated. You are who you are because of their time with you, and they live on in you from the learning they provided.

Some, however, stick around. They are the people who help form the real you; they inspire your values and accept you for your authentic self. Time may pass, but they never do. Two of those people I would connect with on my way through Denver. Todd, Ray, and I could be no different from each other, diverse in every way. They are two men who have had a significant impact on my life not because of things we share in common but because of our differences. It's these authentic differences that bound us together like hoops of steel. To understand these two, let me take you back to the first time I met Todd and Ray more than 30 years ago.

When I first met Todd, we had just joined the same fraternity and were headed out to a cookout to celebrate the new members. I was a conservative at the time, a crew team member, in student government, the preppy type who listened to country music and could be stuffy at times, from a small town with small-town values. I hopped a ride with Todd and Ken in Todd's new car. The discussion, barely audible over the blaring Van Halen music, was about wild parties in Kansas City and all that goes with that, big city, party, concert t-shirts, high schools bigger than my hometown, life. You name it, different! For me, what crossed my mind was, *"Is Satan driving me to hell?"*

Well, that friendship went on long after our college days. We lived together in Boston for a while when he was in law school and I was looking for a job. That friendship continues to grow to this day. Todd is always the first to reach out and encourage me when I'm pushing the limits and pick me back up when I stumble. He and Ray, Ken, Andy, and Shannon accept me for me as I do for them. We grow together even in our differences, no matter the years past. My point in this story is to encourage you to reach out to the people and circumstances that are different from you. To approach the world with curiosity to know that everyone has a story and in that story is a lesson that will make you better. If you take the time to listen truly, the story comes alive in you that the human condition is nothing more than a collection of experiences that magically tie us all together. When we take time to listen to others, in some way, it allows us to know ourselves better, know our place in the world better, and eventually give us the courage to share our story.

Returning to the road to purpose:

"Mile High" great times in one of my favorite cities with longtime friends and fraternity brothers, Todd and Ray. Amazing how years may pass but real friendships never do. Friends and brothers for life! Denver, CO

So how do we find our purpose? A qualifier: I'm convinced that our purpose in life has been with us since birth and simply needs to be discovered. For me, it was as simple as looking back over my life, recalling those times that were the most significant, and asking myself when was I at my best.

To determine your purpose, follow these five simple steps:

Step 1: Look back on your life and identify the most impactful stories, those memories you know in detail and can't shake. The times you were in flow.

Step 2: Pick three to five stories, good or bad. What was their impact? Write them down.

Step 3: Look for and underline patterns in your stories.

Step 4:   Look at your life today. What are you doing today that align with your stories?

Step 5:   Pull it all together in a purpose statement and refine it until it feels right to you and until it gives you clarity.

Your purpose says is a statement of your beliefs, what you are passionate about, what you do better than anyone else, and because of this, you bring value to other people by simply being you. When you do this, the universe falls in place. It's not always easy, but it is always right, it feels right, and you know you are in the right place.

Three Key Signposts Along the Road to Purpose

1.   We often try to live what we think our purpose should be and, in turn, suffer for it.
2.   Talent is our purpose in action. Identify times of flow, and do more of that.
3.   Open your heart to who you are, not what you think you should be.

Chapter 6

Authentic You

"What stands in the way becomes the way."

—Marcus Aurelius

To this point, we have talked about knowing ourselves, who we are at our core, what makes us who we are, and what we bring to the world. We talked about our values, those filters by which we live our lives. We talked about our purpose, why we do what we do, and why it matters to those around us. We talked about our talent, that one thing that we do so well that we enter states of flow when we are doing it. We also talked about getting out of our own way so that we can be the absolute best we can be. About overcoming the voices in our heads that tell us we can't, the fears that keep us inside our comfort zones, the idea of an optimistic view of the world, and our ability to control our destinies by controlling our thoughts.

Being yourself is bringing that together and is the foundation for being the best you can be. In a world where we feel pressured to be what others want us to be at work, in our social groups, in our peer groups, in our mind sometimes, or driven by what we see on social media, it's important to note that the best you is always *you*. The authentic you. Nowhere does courage play a more significant role than in being yourself. So, what do I mean by "be yourself"?

As a marketer, we built brands or marks that make an impression on the minds of those who would potentially buy our products or services. A brand is simply an emotional connection between a product and the person using the product. Your brand is no different; it is the real and authentic you. Your brand connects at an emotional level with those who you associate with—your family, your friends, your clients, your classmates, your community—everyone. It is you, the real you, and an essential ingredient in living a life of meaning and purpose. After a lifetime building brands for companies, what I learned was that my brand was what the client, my friends, family, and all those I came in contact with were buying. The product was simply the reason for the interaction, but in the end, it was me they were buying.

The difference with people is that often we lose track of who we are by giving in to the fear of rejection, by believing that if we are who we are that people will not like us, not respond to us, and in turn, we will end up alone. In the companies we work for, we often get caught up in politics to fit in. The higher we get in an organization, the more we are often expected to adapt to the point of giving up who we are simply to protect a great job with a substantial paycheck. I saw this happen in every company I worked for and feel bad for those who traded fulfillment from a dream they held deep in their hearts for security in the company they worked for.

It also often happens in our social groups, like churches, fraternities, communities, and other places where a person's position dictates their value. Crazily, it's as if we are back on the school playground, nervous we will be chosen last for the dodgeball game at recess. It's no different as adults, only the playground is work or school or our social group and on and on. So often, we give up our true self for others and, over a long period, lose that identity that we were born to share. So, if being our authentic self is what people want from us, why is it that we walk away from who we are? If knowing that our brand is what people want to buy, why is it that we feel a need to take a career or join a group for the prestige or power even though it most often isn't a good fit for our brand?

The road to purpose brought to light not only the question of my brand but that of my story: What was it? Did it make me unique? Who was I to the outside world? After decades of creating brands for products and the mind-numbing process that sometimes occurred getting ideas past corporate department heads, so often those brands ended up watered down and, in a way, I became watered down as well. It's not like this happened overnight—more like a little unnoticeable amount each day until, eventually, you wake up and you no longer know who you are. Next thing you know, you stop knowing what promise you bring to the world. That's a horrible place to be, and I am sure it had a lot to do with the deep despair I would find at times working in those companies. I know this because I lived a life where my brand could change depending on who was consuming it, and that can be exhausting. It often created imposter syndrome, and quite frankly, it was never sustainable.

What exactly is bringing your brand to life in an authentic way? Often, it comes from merely living your life and the values you picked up through those experiences.

Brand You

An authentic brand is one that delivers on the promise it makes. For a personal brand, your genuine brand is where your values, purpose, and talent come together in service to others. Our brand is how we represent ourselves to others. It is proof that we are living our purpose. Our brand simply answers the question, "What do others say about us when we are not around?" Whether you are an individual, own a company, or work for someone else, your brand determines if others are willing to work with you, a critical factor in your personal and professional success. How do we bring that to life in a personal brand?

First, it's a formal process, and like anything else that's important, write it down. The steps are simple, yet living it can be difficult, and writing it down commits you to take action.

Second, follow a simple process:

1.   Discover your brand,
2.   Develop your brand,
3.   Communicate your brand, and
4.   Protect your brand.

Your brand is the perception of who you are and what you stand for based on the consistency of your words and actions. Your brand represents your value to others. It is your promise to friends, family, associates, members of your social club, employees, and customers that they can count on you. Your brand, once developed, must be communicated to the world in your thoughts, words, and deeds and at all costs must be protected. I've known people who have spent a lifetime building a brand only to destroy it in 30 seconds with an off-color remark or action or response that was out of line.

Your brand is your most valuable asset and deserves the priority as such. A clear and concise knowledge of who we are results in "living our authentic self." It ensures that we are "walking the talk" in our actions and building trust and confidence in our relationships, and it provides the example for others to do the same in their own lives. In the end, business and personal life are all about human interaction. Being our authentic self allows others to know who we are and what to expect, and in so doing, it builds the trust and respect required to form healthy relationships in our business and personal lives.

Your brand is the promise that you bring to the world. It is how you deliver on your purpose. The road to purpose made it clear that being yourself, your authentic self, and living your brand every day with those you impact, will prepare you for a life of meaning and purpose.

Personal Responsibility

The key to being authentic is to own everything about who we are and the actions we take. To protect our brand is to take personal responsibility for living our brand promise in everyday life. Doing this is often difficult: We will stumble, come up short, or not live up to the expectations of others at some point in our lives. Taking responsibility for ourselves is a natural part of living a purpose-driven life and is critically important to build trust and credibility with those around you. When we do stumble, we must own it, own the actions we took, learn from them, and move on.

It seems that every time we turn on the news, someone is blaming someone else for a problem society is facing. We are living in a culture of blame, and nothing destroys your brand more than getting caught up in the blame game. By blaming others, you give away your power to them and, in turn, never achieve your goals. By using your situation as an excuse, you give in to that excuse and hold yourself prisoner by that situation. When you don't take full responsibility, when you fail to own it, make excuses, blame others, or fail to let go of the past, that becomes your brand. Is that what you want?

That is what I did in the days that followed leaving my company. I stopped being true to my brand. I started to blame others for my situations, make excuses for why it turned out the way it did, and hold nasty grudges for the company and the people who played a part in it. My brand moved quickly from an optimistic can-do person, a victor, to a blaming, angry, excuse-making victim. I took it personally, and even though it made no sense, I let it impact my brand. It's important to note that the situation was not about me—it made no sense—so why was I trying to find sense in all of it? My mother once said to me, *"If you don't stop trying to make sense out of senseless things, you will do yourself and those you are trying to help no good at all."* This thought rings particularly true, especially when you are struggling to be yourself and the world around you is trying to make you something else.

To sum it all up, taking personal responsibility for your life and all that is in it is a decision. You can decide whether you are going to view a situation from an above-the-line perspective or a below-the-line perspective. Will you take a positive, responsible, optimistic, forward-looking view, be a victor? Or will you approach the world with blame, excuses, negative, and a view of scarcity as a victim? It's entirely up to you. By taking responsibility for yourself, you take control back, and when you have it again, you can make the changes you need to get what you want.

A simple approach to ensure that you take responsibility for your authentic self is to Think, Believe, Decide, Do, and Celebrate. First, think about your purpose and how to bring it to life in the world. Second, believe that you bring value to the world. Third, decide that you and only you can make the changes. Fourth, do the work to bring it to life. And fifth, celebrate the success that comes from it.

When we take full responsibility for ourselves, our actions, and our results, we take back control of our lives from the situation or people impacting us. When we are in control of our lives, our self-esteem and self-confidence improve. When we have control of our lives, we are happier and operate at a heightened level of awareness, which in turn results in higher levels of performance. So, take responsibility for yourself and for your results, and take back control of your authentic life.

Let Go of the Past to Make Room for the Future

The final step in living an authentic life is to let go of the past and focus on your future. Authenticity is critical to building your brand over time. History is no excuse, and where you come from has nothing to do with where you can go, so focus forward. I know this comes across as cold and lacking in empathy. I also know that people can do horrible things to other people, and by no means am I discounting that in any way. What I do know is that holding on to that pain holds you back, and letting go of it frees you to become your best self. I know firsthand the distress this can cause to the relationships that are important to you.

Since the road to purpose, I have had the privilege of working with some very talented young people, young people who are on their own for the first time in their lives. They have an overwhelming responsibility to succeed, fit in with their peers, belong, and persevere. They are young people who are often pushed to be what others think they should be versus what they truly want to be. What I have seen is an entire generation that, on paper, is successful. Inside, however, they are empty, unhappy, and feel like they have no control over their own lives. They believe that they must choose between following their passion and following the money—often resulting in low self-esteem, motivation, and feelings of worthlessness. I've seen this evolve into depression, anxiety, substance abuse, and suicide. My point is that young adults and quite frankly all of us, no matter our past, no matter who influences us, no matter what we think others want from us, are responsible for choosing our path and the results we get. Knowing full well that it can be difficult at times, especially with people you love, pushing back and chasing your idea of success is up to you. If it is to be, it is truly up to me.

We also know that people who influence us and others that we have placed our trust in can impact us in unintentional ways. Often to protect us from making severe mistakes growing up, the protection backfires, resulting in lower self-esteem, self-confidence, and self-concept in ways these people never intended.

These things, people, situations, and words are often detrimental to our long-term potential if we allow the thought to become who we believe ourselves to be. The good news is that we can decide to remove those thoughts and replace them with new ones, to tell ourselves that we will no longer listen to those lies or that we will let go of those times in our lives that negatively impacted us.

The best way to get rid of the empty lies is to forgive. Forgive those who did you wrong, intentionally or unintentionally. Openly forgive them, say it out loud to yourself, or better yet, say it directly to them in person or a letter. Forgiving others releases you from living that pain over and over again. Forgiving others frees you to move on with your life, no longer burdened by the excuses and blame you have used to hold yourself back.

The most important person or situation you need to forgive is YOURSELF. Yes, you. We have all said, did, or didn't do things that we are embarrassed by, that we are ashamed of, that we wish didn't happen. Often, our most prolific critic is ourselves, and we use that negative self-talk to hold us back to sabotage the very success to which we aspire.

Here is the point: What you did, said, didn't do, or didn't say in the past is, well, in the past. There's not a thing you can do about it, so forgive yourself, learn from it, don't do it again, and move on. Forgiving yourself and forgiving those who did you wrong is a crucial decision you must make if you are to move past it, move forward, and move on. You owe that to yourself; you owe that to the world. I know this firsthand, and in later chapters, I will share with you a burden I had carried with myself for over 20 years, a thought, an action that I finally forgave myself for after the road to purpose, forgiveness that launched me to where I am today. It's forgiveness that allowed me to share that experience with others suffering from the same shame, guilt, and life not lived fully.

The road to purpose showed me that a secret to living up to our full potential is to decide to be our authentic selves. To build, live, and protect our unique personal brand. To take responsibility for our success and to set ourselves free through the forgiveness of others and ourselves. Being our authentic self is the only way to live the life we were born to live, one in service to others, a life of meaning and purpose.

Three Key Signposts Along the Road to Purpose

1. Your brand is what makes you unique in a crowded world.
2. Be your authentic self, and embrace your own story.
3. Be a victor. Take responsibility for your life and forgive others—no excuses, no blame.

Chapter 7

Get Up and Get Going

*"The only thing standing between you and your goals
is the bullshit story you keep telling yourself as
to why you can't achieve it."*

—Jordan Belfort

Knowing ourselves, getting out of our own way, being authentic, taking advantage of our talents, a little grit, and a lot of grace are foundational to living our best life. Surrounding ourselves with people who know us and love us just the way we are, who drive us to be our very best and accept nothing less, is what guarantees that we are living our own authentic lives. Everything we have talked about so far means nothing without action. Brian Tracy says that *"goals without action are fantasies."* Relationships without action are shallow and energy-burning. Careers without action are soul-sucking and usually end in layoffs or leaving your company altogether. Universities without ethics are student factories and can lead to entire generations lost. Financial goals without action are bankruptcy, and on and on.

If we are to reach our full potential, we must take action by first grounding everything we do in service to our purpose. Purpose will then allow us to visualize where we want to go and help us put a system in place to get us there. Time will be our biggest enemy, wisdom will be in short supply, and from time to time, our emotions will get the best of us. If we are to realize greatness, we need to prepare, but just as important is to simply "get going," to take the first step if we are to find the life we desire.

My life before I set out on the road to purpose proved this to be true. Like so many corporate types, I put a lot of work into goal-setting, vision, planning, and all the rest of it. It's an effort that takes place every year to present information to senior leaders have to get funding for the following years' projects. Usually, the completed plans sit on a shelf until the process starts all over again the next year. This meaningless and mundane process can be soul-sucking, more for the activity than for the actual results that it produces.

The process itself can be valuable if it's used throughout the year. I have found that family businesses tend to actually use these plans to make educated adjustments over the course of the year. Get going all starts with knowing where you want to end up.

Know What You Want

When you think BIG, your problems become small. When you think big and have clarity in the long-term goal you want to attain, you can then get to work breaking the journey into smaller parts, actions that in and of themselves are small but together create results that would feel unattainable. Having absolute clarity in what we want to achieve, and knowing how it aligns or delivers on our purpose is the first step. Knowing what we want helps us focus our time on what matters most. Knowing what we want is merely setting and achieving goals that point us in the direction of living a life of meaning and purpose. Brian Tracy, a well-known author and business coach, says that "goals are the master skill of success," the one skill that makes all success possible. Let's take a look at four critical steps in defining what we want: clarity, a positive mindset, balance, and taking action.

There is a direct correlation between clarity of what you want in life and how likely you are to get it. Do we have goals that are so clear that an eight-year-old would understand? Do we have a plan and a target for completion? Absolute clarity and focus are essential to goal achievement. As the saying goes, "If you don't know where you are going, you will most likely end up somewhere else."

Absolute clarity in what you want will ensure that your final destination is the one that you intended. One way to ensure clarity is to apply the S.M.A.R.T. approach to goal-setting. S.M.A.R.T. goals are specific, measurable, aligned, realistic, and time-bound. Specific: What exactly is it that you want to achieve? Measurable: How will you know you have reached your goal? Aligned: Does the goal align with who you are and what you stand for? Realistic: Do you believe that you can achieve the goal? Time-bound: When do you plan to achieve your goal? Clarity is critical if you are to get what you want.

Next up is a positive mindset. Do we think about our goals all the time and allow our brains to work on ways to achieve them? Psychologists have known for years that those who are continually thinking about what they want and how to get it are happier, more in demand, and have a higher rate of success. They can visualize success and its impact on the people they hold dear. Setting and achieving goals drives higher levels of self-esteem, self-image, and self-confidence and leads to the achievement of even higher goals in the future.

Living a balanced life is the third step and the secret to living a fulfilling and successful life. We have all heard that "variety is the spice of life" and goal-setting is no different. Balance in goal setting should address all major areas of your life, including your wellness, relationships, work, wealth, wisdom, and impact on the world. Set clear goals for your career and income both for the short term and long term. Know what you want from your relationships with family and friends. Make sure you are focusing on building a sound mind, body, and spirit. Plan for your future, and make sure that you have investments in place that allow you to become financially independent in your later years.

Neglecting one area of your life will impact all others. I have known many who put all their eggs in the "career" basket, later to find their family life in shambles, with health problems, and with a spiritual emptiness that came full-circle to destroy their career, leaving them with nothing but despair and crisis. Ensure that you have at least one primary goal in each area of your life, and you will find that all parts will work together in harmony toward success.

You will have one goal that will impact on all the other goals. I like to call this your Apex goal. Identify the one goal that has the most significant impact on your life, the one goal that is most important to you, motivates you, and makes you happy. Work on this goal first with complete focus before moving on to the next.

Your primary goal should be a stretch but one you believe is achievable. Let me say that again: that *you* believe is achievable. No one else's opinions matter—only yours. Write it down. Let me say that again, WRITE IT DOWN. A Harvard study found that only three percent of us have written goals, and those with written goals achieved levels of success equivalent to the remaining 97 percent combined. Writing down your goals programs the subconscious mind and energizes you to focus on actions to achieve it.

Finally, take action. We all know that a goal without a plan of action never gets done. It becomes a dream, a wish, a fantasy. To take action and focus our efforts, we need a plan. For some reason, the word "plan" scares people away. It feels daunting, rigid, and something to procrastinate to the end. Here is the crazy thing: A plan is nothing more than a to-do list, prioritized and put in chronological order. That's it. It is merely breaking your goal down into smaller tasks and identifying the systems and rituals to achieve a little progress every day. By doing this, you will find that it will make each step easier to accomplish, the process will become more enjoyable, and it will be something you can work on a little bit each day. Taking on smaller tasks over and over again will form habits that make success more likely to stick with you for the long haul.

How many of you have set a goal to lose weight only to gain it back once your goal is attained? Forming habits will increase the likelihood of a lifestyle change and, in turn, long-term success. Tony Robbins, one of the world's most successful life coaches, says that progress or achieving small, incremental steps each day is the catalyst for happiness. James Clear considers habits to be the compound interest of self-improvement, and by putting these habits in motion by taking action, you will take your goal from a mere hope or dream to the catalyst that will change your life.

Without a plan, goal-setting has no value. Without a plan of action, all that you want to achieve will be out of reach. A clear and concise knowledge of what we want is critical to ensure that we are focused on leading a meaningful and successful life. Simply knowing what you want has never really been the problem. Doing the work to achieve what you want is what separates the successful from those who simply exist and fumble their way through life. "Knowing what you want" is the roadmap for getting where you want to go and for making your impact on the world. Knowing what you want and doing the work to get it done will ensure that you live a successful and energized life grounded in purpose. All of this, of course, takes time and an understanding of how to bring those actions to life.

Get a Grip on Time, Skills, and Emotions

Let's explore and add "prioritizing your time" to the equation for a happy and successful life. Time is our most precious resource, the great equalizer for all of us, no matter our background. Time wasted is time gone, never to get back. Time used correctly, however, ensures that we are working on the right things to achieve our most important goals. I have experienced the importance of managing time myself with my coaching clients. Time is by far the most significant stressor my clients face; more specifically, there's "not enough time." It's a simple fact of life that there is never enough time to get it all done. Just like most of us, successful people don't get it all done either, but they have learned how to focus on getting the most important things done in the time they do have.

So, how exactly do we get the most out of the limited time that we do have to achieve our greatest dreams and, in turn, reach our full potential?

Number one, you must first take responsibility for managing your time. If you are continually making excuses for "not having enough time" or accepting that you will always be behind, then you will. If you decided to make managing your time a priority and visualized yourself completing your most important tasks first, you would find that to be your reality. Time, like all other decisions, is all about having the right mindset, taking responsibility for your own time, and moving forward.

Second, there is never enough time to do everything, but there is always enough time to do the most important thing. What is your most important goal, that Apex goal that has the most significant impact on your success? Focus on achieving this goal first until it's complete before moving on to the next one.

Third, do you know where you spend your time in a typical day? On average, we waste almost half our day doing things that don't matter. I learned this the hard way, and thanks to my business coach, I got ahold of it quickly before it could do much damage. When I left the relatively planned corporate life to start my own company, time was what stressed me out the most. After completing a simple exercise my coach had provided me, I realized that I was wasting time on things that didn't matter instead of focusing on getting clients for my new business. It wasn't apparent at first because those other things, well, they took a couple of minutes here and there throughout the day. After the exercise, 40 percent of my time was doing just that—wasting time—in two-minute intervals.

Here is the simple exercise my coach provided to me to help me better understand just where my time was going. She had me track my time for a week in 15-minute increments from the time I woke up until the time I went to bed. At the end of the week, I would then group my time into six or so categories and determine the percent of the time that I spent in each category. I would then identify those activities that helped me move toward my most important goal of "getting clients."

You have to be honest with yourself, and knowing how you spend your time is the first step. My coach had me do exactly this, and a 90-hour workweek soon became 40. With that, my life changed considerably.

A great time management process starts with planning. One minute of planning is said to save 10 minutes of execution. Plan your year at the end of the prior year. Plan your week the weekend before. Plan your day the night before. Prior planning programs your brain to start working on your most important activity first. Something I have found to help do this advanced planning of time is a tool called a "block schedule." This strategy requires a commitment from you to work at scheduled times on significant tasks that deliver on your most important goal. Your ability to create and carve out these blocks of high-value, highly productive time is central to your ability to make a significant contribution to your work and your life.

The best way to plan is to make a list and prioritize it. A prioritized list focuses your efforts on achieving your most important goal first. To prioritize your list, first, apply the 80/20 rule to your list: 20 percent of the tasks that you do will produce 80 percent of your results. We all believe that everything we do is essential, but in fact, most of what we do is not.

Once we have identified what is important, it's time to prioritize. An excellent method for this is to determine what is urgent and what is important and make those tasks your highest priority. Priority 2 tasks are those that are important but not urgent; they must be completed but can be pushed back for a while. The remainders are neither important nor urgent and should be delegated to others or simply discarded altogether. An unimportant task like talking with a friend or a hobby may not help you move toward your goals, but they are enjoyable to you and can be worked in when time allows.

Now that you have a plan, simply get rid of all the noise, the stuff that has no impact on your life and carry very little if any consequences if you don't complete them. Life is not always so simple, and with it comes noise, including priorities that are on other people's lists. The first comes when your boss, a customer, or a fellow student delegates project work to you. By definition, this is important because the consequences of not performing the task can be severe. The question to ask is, "Is it urgent?" Not all tasks are urgent, and your ability to understand the timing of the task is key to your success.

Similar but different are other people in your life delegating their work to you. In some instances, this may be important and, most likely, not urgent. Learning to say no altogether, or with a condition or by postponing the task, is one of the best time management skills you can put in place. Have you identified the noise in your day, the things that take up a lot of time yet contribute nothing to your success?

Finally, take the first step. Ask yourself, "What is the most valuable use of my time right now?" Share your goals and priorities action plan with your manager, a mentor, your coach, a classmate, or an accountability buddy. Take the first step and focus on your most important task until it is complete. When you have control of your time, you have control of your life. Taking control of your life will improve goal achievement. Goal achievement leads to improved self-esteem, which in turn inspires you to contribute more to those around you, resulting in a more fulfilling and happy life.

With a good grip on time, we must apply wisdom to our lives. Wisdom is simply adding experience to knowledge and using prior learning to present opportunities. Long gone are the days when we can simply learn a trade or profession and expect those skills to see us through to retirement. Our world today is quickly changing, and if we are not moving forward at an accelerated pace, then we are falling behind. Our ability to open our minds and find learning in all of our experiences, through traditional means, nontraditional means, and our everyday search for meaning and purpose, is critical if we are to reach our full potential.

All successful people spend their free time learning. Learning takes time. We all go through four steps when we learn something new. Gordon Training International created the four stages of competence in the '70s that apply to this day. While they used different terms, the steps are similar: 1. we don't know what we don't know, 2. we know what we don't know, 3. we know what we know, and 4. habit or the application of a set routine over and over again until it occurs subconsciously.

The single most important way to ensure that we are reaching our full potential is to commit ourselves to a lifetime of learning, especially in our chosen field. The great news is that any one of us can apply this secret to our success. Learning also helps us position ourselves as experts. People pay well for experts and, more importantly, sharing wisdom allows us to become much better mentors, managers, and coaches to others.

So, what do we need to do to use lifelong learning to ensure our success?

First, we must have clarity in exactly what we want and set clear goals to achieve it.

Second, we must be curious. What have you always been interested in but never took the time to learn? Take a look online and research a topic that interests you. Determine the skills that you will need to achieve your goals.

Third, be honest with yourself. Do an accurate assessment of yourself and identify the weaknesses that could get in the way of you achieving your goals. What skills will you need to grow and improve? Your weakest skill determines your success and limits your ability to reach your full potential.

Fourth, determine the one most important power that you will need to achieve your goal, then tackle that one first. You can make more progress by going to work on the one skill that is holding you back more than any other. Now that you know the skill that is holding you back, where might you look for learning to help you conquer it? I have found mentors, coaches, teachers, friends, clients, and competitors are all great sources of learning. They don't have to know you or be directly involved in your life; many come from readings, seminars, or sporting events, all modeling the behavior that you desire but not necessarily know. Observe them, listen to their stories, and in particular, the mistakes and successes they have had over a lifetime. Have an open mind; surround yourself with diverse people who are different than you. Study successful people and learn how they achieved greatness and mirror it. Yes, I said do what they did; no reason to reinvent the wheel. If it worked for them, it will work for you too.

One of my biggest mistakes was not taking advantage of simply reading in my field before the road to purpose. Today, I get up an hour and a half early every morning to read. I have found that this time allows me to digest a book in my field every week. For me, that equates to about 54 books a year compared to the average of one book a year by most people. That edge makes a big difference in your ability to apply the learning to deliver value to your students and clients.

Many of my virtual mentors like Brian Tracy, Tony Robbins, John Maxwell, Joel Osteen, Simon Sinek, and others recommend turning off the radio in your car and using the time for learning through Audible, podcasts, and other mobile tools. I have also found that listening to podcasts, Ted Talks, or other online audio programs during workouts helps me perform those workouts better. Both not only replace the monotony with learning but also inspire you to focus and perform at accelerated levels, making both driving and exercising a lot more enjoyable.

Teaching others is, by far, my most favorite and soul-fulfilling way to learn. Many of you know that I spend my work and volunteer time coaching, training, and mentoring high-performing business leaders and young people—businesses and individuals who are very good at what they do but know, with a little outside help, that they can be significant contributors. What you may not know is that those relationships and the learning that comes through them go both ways. I often find myself leaving our time together better than when I started. I often learn more in our sessions than I teach. The relationships and the learning that comes through them, usually through vulnerable and transparent discussions, has become the joy of my life. By learning through teaching, I have found that learning gives back and helps you grow and reach your potential as well.

Take a university course, learn a trade, or get that degree you have always wanted. Attend as many conferences or workshops as you can, or join a social media group with other like-minded individuals. Nothing is more impactful than hearing from a person who is an expert in their field. It also allows you to have discussions with people who have similar interests to you to share best practices or make lifelong connections. I have found this dialogue to produce learning that is greater than the sum of its parts, learning that often leads to more questions that, in turn, leads to more learning.

Approach the world from a growth perspective, see a learning opportunity in every experience, good and bad. Be positive and look at your life as a learning lab. Push yourself to places you have never allowed yourself to go before. Face and find ways to overcome your fear, the fear that makes you uncomfortable. Push through it, and you will be surprised by what you find on the other side. The learning in and of itself is unimaginable; the learning about yourself and your capabilities to overcome is priceless. Learn from yourself, take chances, make mistakes, learn, adjust, and move on. Convert knowledge into something useful, wisdom. Just knowing it without experiencing it has little value.

For learning to provide value, you must apply it. The application of learning and the experience from it, combined with the knowledge, is what leads to success. In the spirit of Kaizen, which is a Japanese term for continuous and never-ending improvement, improvements often occur in small increments that eventually lead to significant changes over time. It's in these changes and the additional learning that comes from the journey that substantially impacts your life.

Finally, getting a grip on your emotions is critical if you are to ever get beyond average. To this point, we have talked about knowledge and skills to build intellectual capacity, yet nothing impacts success more than your emotional intelligence. Emotional intelligence begins with learning to negotiate with your overactive brain. If success lives on the other side of our comfort zones, then what is keeping us from getting there is our mind.

We get in our own way all the time. Often, that comes with a price—self-sabotage, fear of success, and many other ways we stop ourselves from getting what we want. Have you ever been right on a position but wrong on how you delivered it, regretting the words you used? Have you been angered by a friend and fired off a hateful text, thinking, "I'll show her to regret it later"? Both acts are most likely signs of low emotional intelligence and can have a long-lasting impact on both the relationships and your ability to realize success. If you want a successful and happy life, then you better get your EQ in check!

EQ, or emotional quotient, is the flipside of the more commonly known IQ, or intelligence quotient. EQ is our ability to manage our emotions, understand the situational impact, and communicate better to improve our relationships with others. Studies show that EQ is responsible for over 75 percent of our success. At work, that means effective, high-performing teams, happier, more engaged employees, and a work environment that creates "purpose-filled" and happy lives. Managers with high EQ produce more, influence change, and lead more engaged teams, resulting in higher profits and lower turnover. Employees with high EQ enjoy their work lives more, take more initiative, feel ownership in their work, and get promoted more often. From my own experience, I have enjoyed the success and the challenges that have resulted from both high and low EQ in my career and have learned that high EQ is an essential variable in a successful life.

The road to purpose showed me the power you have over your reaction to stress by merely getting rid of the pressure before you react. The journey started with anger, then depression, emptiness, and finally, purpose. Allowing myself to go through that process allowed me to approach the world with a clear mind. I know what you are thinking: I can't take a random road trip every time I get angry and am about to go off on someone. No, you can't, but you can take a walk around the block, count to ten, take deep breaths, or commit to not responding to emails and texts right away, giving yourself time to cool down.

The first step is knowing yourself and your triggers, then understanding the position of the other person. A person with high EQ senses how others are feeling before they react. When a person can read the facial cues of others and gauge their reactions, it becomes easier to steer the conversation or goals in such a way that will be pleasing to everyone. Emotional intelligence helps in relationships as well as day-to-day interactions with everyday people at work or in school. People with high EQ notice and help others.

Most people are so preoccupied with their tasks and goals that it can be easy to forget that others may need help. However, taking the time to notice and be mindful of others is a trait synonymous with emotional intelligence. So when people on these people's teams are struggling, they catch it and address it before productivity is lost.

People with high EQ are also good motivators of self and others. When you can empathize and be mindful of others' problems and needs, the next step is to translate that understanding into solutions targeted to that person. This ability can transform a good leader into an exceptional one. People with high EQ are self-motivated, too. It's not just about having the ability to empathize with and motivate others. Emotional intelligence is synonymous with knowing yourself. When others see their leader continue to produce effectively, conquer their weaknesses, and fight through difficult situations, it encourages them to work hard for a leader they trust.

You may have heard that your IQ never really increases after reaching a certain age, and that is mostly true. Even though you learn and grow throughout adulthood, your intelligence quotient develops during adolescence. Your EQ, on the other hand, is learnable, and you can improve it throughout your adult life. Understanding your EQ and setting your baseline for self-awareness, self-regulation, motivation, empathy, and social skills is the first step. Then, with practice and the support of a good coach or mentor, you can shift your thinking and, in turn, build new habits that will improve your life.

Sound Mind, Body, and Spirit

I've never been one who believed in the whole hocus pocus, meditation thing. Never really understood why anyone would want to sit around and just think about not thinking. Who has time for that, anyway? What the road to purpose has taught me through endless hours alone in a car is that we must clear our mind of all the noise, the racing thoughts, and most often, limiting beliefs that keep us from living a fulfilling and prosperous life. What I found was that acknowledging those thoughts and then dismissing them as if they were a feather floating in the wind allows your mind to calm, and in the calmness, you find peace in the present versus dwelling on the past or worrying about the future. The crazy thing is that when I have peace, new, positive thoughts fill my head, and new ideas fall upon me like rain. Mindfulness, as I found out, empties the mind of all the noise to make room for the new thoughts that moved me forward.

Today, I have a very disciplined morning routine that begins with turning on the small coffee maker in my office, followed by going through a priming routine created by Tony Robbins. In priming, I do think but about specific things at an in-depth but focused level. Priming starts with a necessary deep-breathing exercise, combined with pumping my arms to get my body moving. I follow that with three minutes of gratitude for people and situations that have impacted my life in some way. Next is the practice of a technique called a body scan, where I visualize energy running through my body head to toe, healing my mind, body, and spirit over and over again. Once I feel that energy in my body, I send it out to people in the form of prayer or intentions for those struggling. Finally, the third step is to focus on three goals to complete for the day.

The second part of my morning ritual is journaling a little more detail around gratitude, intentions, and goals that I visited in the priming exercise. Journaling, in a way, is getting all those thoughts in my head out on paper where I can better address them. Some have said journaling is therapy on paper, and I tend to agree.

I finish my morning by reading a book in my field for an hour or so. I find this combination of emptying my head, being grateful, then thinking about my day and the essential people in my life to create a start to the unstoppable day. Starting this way makes it hard to have a bad day, and if you do, merely following the daily goals seems to bring it all back together.

The rest of the morning includes a 45-minute cardio workout each day to get the endorphins up and a healthy breakfast with my wife before I head to the office. I also have an evening routine to "bookend" my day and to ensure that I don't spend all my time at the office. I usually finish my day with planning the next around

6 p.m., having dinner with my wife, and watching a little TV while I drink a cup of chamomile tea before I head up for a bit of solitude then get my seven to eight hours of great sleep.

Finally, all of this takes energy, and a lot of it. It also takes courage, a lot of it, plus brainpower. The most significant learning on the road to purpose is that you must first take care of yourself, your mind, your body, and your spirit, to be of value to others. Mindfulness, health, and a positive outlook are the most critical tools for a long and happy adventure.

What I learned on the road to purpose is that all the planning in the world, the goals, dreams, aspirations, are all a big waste of time if you don't take action, if you don't take the first step, if you don't get going. To do that, you must first know your purpose. You must know where your vision lies and how to get there, and you must know your goals and plans. You must figure out the roadblocks and detours along the way, like time, knowledge, wisdom, and your own emotions that can cause you to crash and burn.

Like everything else you have read so far, it all starts with taking the first step, and that requires you to move your feet. That requires you to think, to believe in yourself, and to do the work if you want results. So many forget the work part then write this all off to yet another thing they wanted to do but didn't get done. It's in that first step that you find success, that you find confidence and that you find purpose. It's all up to you.

Three Key Signposts Along the Road to Purpose

1. Know what you want, visualize success, set goals, and make a plan of action.
2. Identify what you need to know to achieve your plan, and get learning.
3. Energize your mind, body, and spirit to get it done and get going.

SECTION III

RESOLVE TO LOVE YOURSELF

"Loving ourselves through the process of owning our story is the bravest thing we will ever do."

—Brené Brown

Chapter 8

Family And Friends Forever

"Sometimes we have to leave home in order to find out what we left there and why it matters so much."

—Shauna Niequist

After more than a month on the road, I was beginning to have a pretty good idea of who I was as a person, what I stood for, and what I was born to be. I started the journey angry, hurt, let down, and disappointed. Through the lives of the people I met and their hospitality, I began to see a better way, one of hope and optimism. A life of meaning and purpose. If they could overcome their challenges, then so could I. If they could decide to move forward, then I would too.

It helped that I had a lot of time in the car by myself to contemplate where I had been, where I was, and where I wanted to go. With all that time, I started to realize that I had so much more to give. What I learned is that if your heart is full of anger, then your brain has no chance of helping you find your own way forward.

My transformation was taking shape. I was starting to like myself in ways I hadn't ever permitted myself to do before, yet there was still a ways to go to reinforce my newfound wisdom. For one, I would need to put a system in place that ensured that I didn't go back to the way I had lived my life before the road to purpose.

That system would have to focus on building my resilience and the energy needed to live my own life of meaning and purpose. I would also need to surround myself with family and friends, be grateful for who I was, and start using my talents to give back to the world. By doing this, by living a life of meaning, I would, in essence, be wrapping the arms of grace around my own body in a gesture of unconditional love so that I in turn could love others.

Safe and Sound

Love, for most of us, starts with family, both the family we are born into and the family we have chosen along the way. They are those people who love us for who we are, push us to be our best selves, celebrate with us, and consult us when we need it. It's people like our friends, neighbors, teachers, and for me, my fraternity brothers. Those we volunteer with, work with, and make a difference with. Those people who come into our lives at precisely the right time for the right reason to power us forward.

Many of us are blessed with strong families and find ourselves going back to them for the important things in life, like finding a partner, starting a new job, or buying a company. So often taken for granted, these heroes are steadfast and see us through to the end. They never quite let go, but the good ones do allow us to venture out on our own. Sadly, families like mine are few and far between these days, and we must step in and be there for those who need our support. I can think of no better way to celebrate your family than to share their teachings with others, to help others find the success that our families saw in each of us that is just as real inside each of them.

Returning to the road to purpose:

About halfway through the journey, my path would take me back to where it all started, my hometown. My hometown is where I grew up and learned a lot about life. It was also the very place that I couldn't wait to move out of after graduation from high school. Don't get me wrong, life there was incredible. I had a respected, self-made family who ran a successful family business in town. I was popular in high school and made some of the best friends my life would ever produce. My hometown was a safe place where a kid could make mistakes and learn, where your neighbors watched out for you because they cared. A place where hard work counted and you were accountable for your actions simply because you matter. A place where church on Sunday after a night out on Saturday was perfectly okay. A town where a cold beer after a hard day's work was a way of life. A place where doors were left unlocked and where cars were often left running in front of downtown stores on a cold winter's day to keep the car warm while you did your shopping. I can think of no better place to grow up in than Beloit, population 3,700. Yet inside, I knew I could achieve more, that I could spread my wings and do great things, that the entire world was mine to conquer; that the grass must be greener on the other side.

What I know now is that the most important lesson learned was not in the place itself or in the leaving of that place for something better but in the courage to do so. What I *learned through my parents and their efforts to provide a better life for my family was courage. Courage to lay it all on the line to start a business. Courage to move to a new place and make a life for yourself, a place for taking responsibility to make the community you now call home better. Courage to simply step outside your comfort zone to see what's on the other side. And later, the courage to return home, to recharge after a devastating career failure, knowing that you would be embraced, picked up, then pushed back out to chase your dreams.*

This part of the trip reminded me that no matter where you go, what you become, who you are, your very "meaning and purpose" has always been with you. Your unique gift from God was most certainly developed in the very place where it all started, your hometown. It became clear to me on this stop that all roads forward often return home on their way to whatever is next. It was on this part of the journey that the safest place on earth made it clear that a theme was developing. The people I had visited all had one thing in common: courage. They had all found happiness by getting past fear, pushing through hardships, sacrificing short-term for long-term rewards, for doing the scary things, never giving up, and in turn, enjoying a better life. Courage, being afraid, and doing it anyway would become even more apparent in the days that followed. The road to purpose had me asking, "Why is it that the road to the future always makes a stop in the past?" "Ad astra per Aspera," getting grounded and reenergized in my most awesome hometown, Beloit, KS

As I rolled into town, a smile began to cross my face as my entire life history began to come back to me like it was yesterday: all the good, the bad, and the ugly. Of finding love for the first time, experimenting with adulthood, friendships that consumed many late nights, and long days on a tractor with my best friend talking about girls, parties, our hopes and dreams, and what life could be. I recalled working for my dad's company, the friends and coworkers who became mentors along the way. Thoughts of times when I was not at my best and other times that became some of my proudest moments all began to come back to me. The hard lessons learned, on things like trust, patience, hard work, and treating people right, all stored deep my heart, became as real as the day they occurred so long ago. Yes, my life flashes before me in detail when I return home, that place where a tiny seed would grow into the man I had become and the meaning and purpose that I possessed. No matter how hard you try to move on, how hard you try to run away, a life of purpose always returns home to be recharged with a sense of quiet confidence that had never left.

Returning to the road to purpose:

As I began the final month of my journey, two words kept coming to mind: "quiet confidence." Words that have shaped my past and without a doubt will be the foundation for whatever comes next, the most significant gift given to me by my parents, the best teachers I know. The lessons are so eloquently brought to life in the final words of my favorite poem, "Desiderata" by Max Ehrmann: "No doubt the universe is unfolding as it should. Therefore, be at peace with God, whatever

> *you conceive Him to be, and whatever your labors and aspirations, in the noisy confusion of life, keep peace in your soul. With all its sham, drudgery, and broken dreams, it is still a beautiful world. Be cheerful. Strive to be happy."*

"Desiderata" lays out a blueprint for a happy life. It talks about telling the truth, respecting others, avoiding bad people, and not comparing yourself to others. It talks about being grateful for what you have and being cautious of business deals but not so much that you close yourself off to opportunity. It says to be yourself, to grow old gracefully, and to love yourself. "Desiderata" confirms that we all have a right to be here and a responsibility to make life better.

Returning to the purpose:

> *As it often does, my return home left me recharged and ready to take on what's next. With all the noise from the past gone, a hearty dose of "getting grounded" and the discovery that my purpose had been with me all along, I prepared to head out to take on the world.*

> *That notion of retirement was also gone and quickly replaced with a vision of giving back; using my talents and life experiences to help others quickly filled the void. Happiness became the goal, and I was going to do it by helping others achieve their goals and make a living doing exactly that. Funny how assisting others in finding happiness helps you make the same—merely*

the golden rule in action! What I learned going back to my hometown was that sometimes the hardest step is the first one and that courage is what it takes to make it.

This part of the trip also reminded me that capitalism and social responsibility could and must live in harmony with each other. My own family had proved that you could start with nothing except love and support, work hard in service to others, and through that success, earn a living. That profit was not something to be embarrassed by but something to do good with in the world. With great opportunity comes great responsibility to help others have a better life.

Later, these lessons would become so clear that what I was to do next was coach, mentor, and be a beacon of hope for others. Kansas had taught me that while this newfound understanding seemed fresh and new, it had been with me all my life. It was on the road to purpose, hanging out with my family, aunts and uncles, that it became clear to me that my success and values worked hand in hand. Together, they brought to life the stories of my family, all living examples that if you treat people right, set high expectations, and are willing to work for it, ANYTHING is possible.

My next stop would be where that small-town boy would go to become a man. My nephews had both followed me to my alma mater, and the youngest was finishing up his degree while I was in town. I had the opportunity to connect with him and his roommates for dinner on my way through town and talk about their experiences. Their stories, not so different from the life I had experienced 30 years ago, were plagued with the same anxiety that I have come to know as an epidemic of this generation.

Returning to the road to purpose:

Each generation brings value to the past. Great time hanging out and talking with my nephew and his housemates at my alma mater, Kansas State. So, impressed with these guys and their parents… No worries, they are well on their way to ruling the world! With Blake and friends, Manhattan, KS

Prodigal Son

My next stop on the road to purpose took me back to the place and the people who kicked off my early adult life. What I had initially thought of as a social club to help me meet people as a new college freshman would later prove to impact my life in a significant way.

My fraternity, Sigma Phi Epsilon, was one of 26 fraternities on campus. It took this small-town boy and made me a man. It taught me how to collaborate with others, how to be a leader, and how to get things done through others. The fraternity taught me the importance of leading a balanced life in service to others. It taught me the importance of maintaining a sound mind, sound body, and sound spirit. It is single-handedly the reason I didn't drop out of school, the reason I graduated and went on to pick up additional advanced degrees. My fraternity taught me that service to others is the only true path to happiness.

SigEp taught me the principles of virtue (Can I trust you?), diligence (Will you do your very best?), and brotherly love (Do you care for me and others?), which, to this day, act as filters for my most important decisions. It provided me with a lifetime responsibility of brotherhood and a group of brothers that console me in bad times, kick me in the ass when I need it, and love and celebrate me no matter what. And when I let career and life get in the way of that balance and wandered away for a while, it was my fraternity that was there with open arms when I found my way back. SigEp is a crucial ingredient in the success that I have experienced since that day so long ago and was there for me 30 years later in my darkest hour when my job was eliminated and this journey began.

Today, the fraternity world is under fire. In a time when the 24-hour news cycle features a few bad actors who are fraternity men in name only, it threatens the very existence of the vast majority of young men who use their experience to serve others and to grow personally. Don't get me wrong, those who commit crimes are evil people and should suffer the full wrath of our justice system for their violent, demeaning, and hideous acts. Hazing, sexual violence, binge drinking, mental health issues, and other cancers facing college students today must end. I have met some true heroes in this space and will share those selfless and inspiring stories in later chapters. I happen to get to see the best in fraternities, the best in people through my volunteer work with SigEp. I see brothers who have taken the high road to fight these cancers plaguing young men in our newest generation. They inspire me and continue to be beacons of hope, a guiding light in my life today.

My fraternity was also my first introduction to "meaning and purpose." We are often introduced to our future at a very young age without a true understanding of what that means. For me at age 18, I knew the words but didn't fully understand the meaning until the road to purpose. At age 51, I finally understood the true power of these words and the impact living them would have. I now realize that through our principles of virtue, diligence, and brotherly love, I had been living "meaning and purpose" all my life without knowing it. It aligned with what my mom and dad had taught me and showed me through their example growing up. In so many ways, my family and my fraternity came together for a reason. SigEp changed my life and set me on a path that would later prepare me to improve the lives of many along the way.

Returning to the road to purpose:

Brotherly love and leadership development were the tools that would change my life. Dear old fraternity, all my life through, I'll love and cherish the memory of you. Should harm betide thouer' will guide me. Sigma, dear Sigma-Phi-Epsilon, true!

The past 50 years of searching for whatever it was that I was looking for would become very clear on this part of the journey. What I thought to be happiness—an impressive career, money, trophies of success, and pleasure—were replaced with the gifts of knowing myself, being myself, and loving myself. It turned out that the gift I had been given through the pain of my career being over had forced me to face life. What I thought was running away from life actually found me running home to where it had always been. The prodigal son had returned to where it all started and, in doing so, found peace of mind in knowing everything was going to be alright. That night, I slept better than I had in months and awoke excited about the adventure ahead as I packed up the car and headed east. With only a few stops left, I was now almost ready to head back home to get started on my new life.

Returning to the road to purpose:

Great seeing my friend and brother Ken on my trip through Kansas City. Ken and I could be no different than each other and come from very different backgrounds. He is the one that brought us all together, cherished our unique selves, and is the glue that has kept the crew together for over 30 years. Ken defines for me the value of Brotherly Love: To be a true friend. To have your back. To intervene when you lose your own way. To help those in need. To be kind to one another. Friends and brothers for life! Country Club Plaza, MO

After a quick lunch with Ken and catching up, I would head on to St. Louis. St. Louis had been home to me on three separate occasions with an incredible company that I had worked at for over 20 years. It was a fantastic company with some of the most talented and inspiring people I have ever known. My time there was full of nothing but great memories as well as some of the most trying times in my professional life, including a hostile takeover by a multinational. Trying times, yes, and while I eventually left, my professional life was formed there, and for that, I am grateful. I'm also grateful for several incredible creative people who became lifelong friends. I would spend the night with Drew and revisit all the glory of St. Louis with those who supported me as I learned to face corporate adversity for the first time.

Returning to the road to purpose:

"Whiskey is water with a soul!" Exploring some of St. Louis' old attractions and a perfect new watering hole featuring 500+ whiskeys and the best BBQ anywhere, BBQ Saloon in the Central West End. On rare occasions, one is lucky enough to experience a time and place where the line between work and play goes away. Reconnecting with past partners and lifelong friends Drew, Jack, Phil, and Tracey, St. Louis, MO

Meaning and Purpose on Trial

Leaving St. Louis on my way to Chicago, I started to think again about how I would fill the remaining weeks on my trip. After all, I was ready to get home and get started but had a few more people I wanted to see. A smile crossed my face as I thought about the year I had worked in Chicago and the people I hadn't seen in over a decade. I started thinking about the great food and good times I would have when a call came in, a call that would break my heart and shorten the remainder of my trip.

As most life journeys often do, I found the road to purpose was not immune to the hills and valleys along the way. I found that even when we have found our purpose, life can still hit rough patches. The biggest one occurred as I was halfway through my second month. I was armed with a strong sense of who I was, a really good sense of meaning and purpose, and knowing what I was going to do with my life when I returned home. The remainder of the trip was for the celebration of the journey and the new me who was emerging from it. It would be full of seeing people, enjoying their company, and sharing my future dreams and aspirations of helping people for a living.

As if by design, just when I thought it would be downhill from that point on, the universe threw me a curveball, as if to say, *Are you sure this is what you want to do with your life? Do you have it in you to truly be vulnerable? To be curious, courageous, and compassionate? Can you handle the human side of taking people through times of distress? Do you really want to do this?*

The stop that never happened was Chicago. On my way, I received a call that no one with a heart ever wants to receive. Another young man, a recent graduate and alumnus of my fraternity, had been hit by a train, and suicide was suspected.

Less than a year earlier, just before starting as a volunteer for the group, that same fraternity had lost a brother to suicide over the holiday break and was still grieving from that experience. The young man had lost his battle with mental illness, and while at home, away from his brothers over the holidays, he had decided to take his own life.

On the outside, he was everyone's friend, loved by all who knew him, and one of those special people who lifted the spirits of everyone in the room when he was around. His death had a considerable impact on his brothers and the university as a whole. Thousands showed up for a candlelight memorial service, and the pain of suicide became very real for the young people on campus in the very prime of their lives getting ready to change the world.

Today, a memorial poker tournament happens each year to raise money for mental health causes in his name. Mental health awareness and prevention programming have been put in place to remove the stigma of this evil disease that has changed the culture at the University of Louisville, a loving community that, through the death of a brother, continues to bring his joy and hope to new students each year. More on this later.

Well, I would later learn that the young man was hit by a train and was in fact a member of the fraternity. He had graduated three years prior but was still known by the seniors in the chapter. A second suicide in less than a year was reason to cut my trip short and get back to my brothers to be there for support, simply to listen and help them talk through the hopelessness of it all—to help them find meaning and purpose, to truly flourish in their own lives and put aside the sadness that so often plagues young people today.

So, if I was going to find my meaning and purpose, if I was called to do and it was going to address the difficulties in young people's lives, I knew that I would first have to be strong myself. The unimaginable pain felt by a group of young men that I care deeply about would test me emotionally to the core.

It brought back memories from my time working with troubled youth early in my career. I remember as a young professional being hell-bent on helping young people as a volunteer in a youth wing of a state psychiatric hospital, leaving each night in tears. The young men, all behind three locked doors, were all under 12 years old and had experienced many suicide attempts and drug addictions. There were a couple who were bullied to the point of killing a classmate. Who can be so sad at 12? I distinctly remember a call to my mother while under distress, talking about one boy in particular who was being sent home to the very place that caused his struggle in the first place. In tears and mad as hell about the decision, I reached out to her to help me understand how I could fix this.

My mother, a clinical social worker, said to me, "Greg, if you don't stop trying to make sense out of senseless things, you're not going to be any good to yourself or those boys either." She went on to tell me that sometimes things are senseless, that there is no answer for why someone else does what they do. That all you can be is support and that what they choose to do is out of your control. That thinking has stayed with me my entire life, and I would need it now more than ever if I was going to survive in the career I chose. I would first have to build strong emotional tolerance for unimaginable pain and, second, understand how human beings process their thinking in search of happiness.

With this in mind, I thought to myself, *If I could not remove the suffering from these young men, then maybe what I could control was helping them find the happiness in themselves. I could help them help themselves if they chose to do the work.*

I began to read on the subject of happiness. My research has since led me to study the work of Dr. Abraham Maslow on basic human needs and Dr. Martin Seligman on authentic happiness. Maslow was perhaps best known for his theory of psychological health brought to life through his hierarchy of needs. Dr. Maslow questioned the current teaching of the time on human behavior and created a new discipline, humanistic psychology, to explain basic human needs through his pyramid model. In this model, Dr. Maslow believed that all human needs begin with basic physiological needs such as food, safety, security, love and belonging, esteem, and finally, self-actualization, loving and accepting yourself. He believed that all human beings begin at the bottom of the pyramid and don't move to the next level until that need is met.

Shortly before his death, Maslow proposed that there was a sixth level to his model, a spiritual one, called transcendence. Transcendence is defined as going beyond oneself, connecting with others and all of humankind, to move from self to society, and to achieve real and long-lasting fulfillment. Contemporary study in psychology and the work of many of today's self-help gurus have built on Maslow's and others' work in human behavior and motivation to make the science more palatable and applicable to those on the journey of self-improvement, enlightenment, and wellbeing. While these ideas may differ slightly, they all conclude that human happiness is directly related to serving each other. That is our human condition; in the end, we are social beings, and together is the only way for us to reach our true potential and find true and authentic happiness.

This final stage I found to be true somewhere in the deserts of Utah along the road to purpose. It became clear to me that we are all unique as individuals, extraordinary and amazing in our own way. We all have great gifts to share with the world. By sharing those gifts and helping others realize their gifts, we can become truly happy. In the end, happiness doesn't come from things, money, prestige, or fame—it comes in playing out the role we were born to play in service to others, or living a life of meaning and purpose. I would finish one last stop before I headed home, a home that would now test my newfound "purpose" and one that I would later realize was my destiny all along.

Three Key Signposts Along the Road to Purpose

1. Often, the search for meaning and purpose is found by returning home.
2. Family is not only the ones you were born with but also the ones you choose.
3. Your purpose will survive all tests over a lifetime.

Chapter 9

The Attitude Of Gratitude

"Be thankful for what you have; you'll end up having more. If you concentrate on what you don't have, you will never, ever have enough."

—Oprah Winfrey

What exactly does it mean to "love yourself"? Love is one of those things that is hard to define. We all see it differently based on our own experiences, life challenges, personalities, and behaviors. It's no coincidence that love is so seemingly undefinable because love, like most emotions, is formed in the emotional center of the brain where no language or logic exists—that same place where loyalty, purpose, and meaning is processed. A vital part of the brain, especially when we are under pressure, the limbic system is what keeps us alive when things go south. It's also that place where fear and limiting beliefs thrive. That in and of itself makes it difficult to define concepts like the emotion of love. We know it's there, just not what it is.

For the purpose of this chapter, I would like to equate love to happiness, especially when it comes to loving yourself. What I mean by this is that when you are doing what you need to do, surrounding yourself with the people who matter most, enjoying bliss and an aura of fulfillment, you are most likely experiencing "love of self." Love of self is way more than the pleasure-seeking actions that we take: That new sports car, the trophy partner, money, fame, and all the other excesses that come with it are not love.

Love of self is doing what you need to do to live your authentic life, doing what you love doing the most, and doing it in service to others. Service is where true happiness occurs, and for me, that is the very time when the love of self is out in front. We are taught at a very young age to be kind to people, to sacrifice for others, and on and on, which is all good advice in moderation. But when we sacrifice ourselves for others over and over again, we will eventually burn out, get bitter, and stop giving. I know because this was me before the road to purpose. Giving to my company, giving to my friends, giving to nonprofits, giving, giving, giving, and what did I get from it? Reorganized out of a job, little help finding a new one, and a lot of despair. All that help had not come back to me like I was promised or at least had negotiated with myself in my head. Despair, anger, and bitterness toward all those who I had helped became the new me. As long as that anger inside existed, I would continue to spiral into various states of depression. Something had to give.

So how do we love ourselves first so that we can love others? First, I believe that finding balance is critical for a happy and fulfilling life. For me, the six crucial areas of balance include wellness, relationships, work, wealth, wisdom, and world. The world is giving back to the human race in some way: the final and most crucial move in living a life of meaning and purpose. If you don't love yourself first, then you will never truly be able to love others.

Giving to self so that you can give to others was a significant change of thinking for me after I returned from the road to purpose. Before, giving everything to others at my own personal expense was destroying me. After the road to purpose, this became clear, and I saw a need to get me right first. I knew that if I wasn't healthy,

I wouldn't have the energy or the credibility with my clients if I didn't first apply the lesson to myself. Further, I would not be of much long-term value to myself or anyone else.

So how do we give to ourselves first, love ourselves first, so that we can, in turn, love others forever? How do we build personal resilience that allows us to flourish, to improve our self-esteem, self-image, and self-confidence to have both the mindset and energy needed to give to others? First, we need to understand what makes us happy, our basic human needs. Second, we should ensure that we are healthy, removing the noise in our lives and being grateful for who we are, where we are, and what we have.

The Gift of Life

We must meet our own basic human needs including building our amazing selves in order to share those gifts with the world. That takes energy, a lot of it. It takes an ability to run into roadblocks and the mindset to get around them. It takes a belief that we are here for a reason and that we and only we can get it done. In short, it takes a sound mind, sound body, and sound spirit to prepare us for the journey of purpose. None of this is new knowledge; the ancient Greeks taught this centuries ago, but today, knowing how and doing what we need to do are not always aligned.

So, what do we mean by a sound mind? A sound mind is the development of knowledge and the experiences to turn that knowledge into wisdom. It's feeding yourself with books, classes, seminars, podcasts, and other tools of learning. It's following up with action and having experiences that bring that knowledge to life, knowing what works, what doesn't, and where there is room for improvement. A sound mind is making sure that you are continually challenging your thinking, being open to new ideas and new ways of doing things, and ensuring that all those neurons are firing as intended. And it's getting help, reaching out to professionals when things just don't seem right so you can find your own way back to bringing good things to the world. A sound mind drives a sound body and a sound spirit. One does not exist without the others.

A sound body then is doing the work to make sure that you are fit and healthy. It is making sure that that you exercise and eat right, that you are getting enough sleep, managing your numbers, and seeing a doctor regularly to ensure that your body is providing everything it needs to your brain, your heart, and other organs to perform at your very best. A sound body looks good, and when it looks good, you feel good. Exercise, especially aerobic exercise, not only grows muscles but produces endorphins and has a direct correlation to your mood and the clarity of your mind.

Sound spirit: I have found this to be the most important of all three and one that creates the pathways for the other two to travel. Sound spirit is inner peace; it's being one with yourself and your thoughts. It's loving yourself and getting rid of the thoughts that are clogging your view of the world. Having a sound spirit is being present and not worried about the future or dwelling on the past. Mindfulness meditation, solitude, a long shower, and running are all practices that can make all the difference in quieting the voices inside your head. Affirmations, or better yet, visualizing the achievement of your goals as if they have already happened, is an excellent way of setting up your day for success. Affirmations can sometimes manifest as lying to yourself, whereas visualizing success around your goal inspires action that, in turn, results in the satisfaction of actually achieving the goals you have set for yourself. It can also be found in prayer and religion and knowing that you are part of a bigger plan.

Simplify Your Life

To be well is to put yourself first, to simplify your life, and to remove all the clutter from it—clutter of all kinds in thoughts, words, environment, workplace, and yes, the people you allow into your space. It's the organizations you belong to and the things you believe.

Often, life gets complicated, and while we continue to add new stuff to it, we never take the time to remove the old, that which no longer helps us become our best self. In fact, that old stuff is often keeping us from it. That process takes time and provides no value, like that person who is always negative and never takes responsibility for their actions. Or that job that you hate going to every day but continue to do so because you know no other way.

To love yourself, you must get rid of the noise in your life that is holding you back, the baggage that is holding you back, the bad habits that are holding you back, all those things that take up time and in turn take away from your life. If you are giving up your time so that someone else can have a simple life, is that fair? Relationships are a two-way street. If it's only moving in one direction, their direction, it's time for a detour. Loving yourself first starts with valuing yourself, and that usually means valuing your time. Managing your time is not cold and rigid; it provides you with more time for the things that are important to you. Be careful that you are not using up this most valuable resource by helping others manage their time at your expense. Time is precious; once it's gone, it's gone.

The importance of time became very real on my final stop visiting my cousin and his family along the Lake Michigan coast in Indiana. They're an amazing family with what seemed to be a non-stop schedule, yet they were all focused on the most important things, like family, career, and positively impacting the world through sustainable agriculture. The universe was once again unfolding as it should, providing this final lesson before I head home. This stop set me up for what would become my life after the road to purpose.

Returning to the road to purpose:

Take one talented family headed by two very smart parents mastering their fields of law and global marketing, add in a Fortune 100 company travel schedule, the excitement and risk of a sustainable farming startup, close community involvement, private school, and a beautiful home on Lake Michigan. Mix well.

Gently fold in three high-energy, very smart, happy, athletic, compassionate, and curious boys, all with different interests, personalities, and schedules. Add a lot of patience.

Top with a lot of fun times, laughter, and sidebar humorous and honest conversations that can only come from youth. Bake for several years.

What you get is a loving, talented family with very different life experiences, very different political views, and very different goals than mine. A family that can have civil discourse, respects your point of view, and loves you for who you are yet helps you think differently about the world. A family that makes you a better person for knowing them. What a world this would be if everyone lived these values. Incredible weekend on beautiful Lake Michigan with cousin Rob, Penny, and family. Ogden Dunes, IN

Gratitude

Loving yourself often starts with getting out of your own way, with accepting you for you and owning the unique things that you bring to the world. Earlier in this book, I used a Marcus Aurelius quote: "What stands in the way becomes the way." Often, eight out of ten times, what stands in the way is you and your thinking. I know that has been especially true for me. Thinking I'm not good enough, smart enough, pretty enough... I'm simply not enough. We all know that not to be accurate, but nonetheless, the voices in our head work overtime to keep us believing these lies.

You know you are a gift from the universe, and loving yourself means you accept who you are as exactly that, a gift. The very best way to ignore the voices is to stop comparing yourself to others and be grateful for the gifts that make you, you. Be thankful for where you are, who is in your life, and what you have achieved. Be grateful for the difficult times that you faced and survived, learned from, recharged, and started again. Gratitude naturally creates the positive thoughts required to make the next move toward our full potential. You will be surprised how being grateful for where you are today leads to even greater things tomorrow.

Now for the hard part. To be grateful is going to require that we let go of the past and focus on the present with an eye to the future. To be truly grateful for who we are (I said it before), we must forgive ourselves for the things we did in the past that are holding us back. Be grateful for the lessons learned and the life you now have because of it, and move on. You are a child of the universe, and that alone is something to be thankful for.

For me, this was one of the most important lessons I learned. Over time, not forgiving myself for my failures eventually led to severe self-doubt, depression, and worse: a notion that I was never good enough, never adding up to the role models around me. That I was average. This notion of being average led to average decisions that held me back. Not taking over the family business because I believed that I wasn't good enough compared to those who I knew in a family business. Thinking that average people don't own companies. Thinking that I would lose the company my father founded.

All of this followed me throughout my career and, in some way, affirmed to me that I wasn't good enough. All of that changed on the road to purpose when I started to realize that I had actually impacted the world and my work in many ways, ways that would have taken my life in a very different direction had I only got out of my own way. The secret was to simply accept myself and stop continually wanting to be someone else or to have what someone else had. Being grateful for what we have is the only way we can truly love ourselves.

Returning to the road to purpose:

Home again, to an incredible life ahead: "It's a funny thing about coming home. Nothing changes. Everything looks the same, feels the same, even smells the same. You realize what has changed is you." —F. Scott Fitzgerald

Happy to be home from the most incredible adventure getting reacquainted with friends, family, and myself. Louisville, KY

Four Key Signposts Along the Road to Purpose

1. The first thing is giving to yourself so that you can give to others.
2. Give yourself a healthy mind, body, and spirit to build a foundation for the future.
3. Clean out the clutter—things, people, thoughts—to make room for the new.
4. Be grateful for who you are and what you have. Be open to opportunities.

Chapter 10

Lead From The Sidelines

*"If I have seen further than others,
it is by standing upon the shoulders of giants."*

– Isaac Newton

I have purposely saved this chapter to wrap up the Resolve to Love Yourself section because I believe that it is the most important one. The very best way to love yourself is to invest in yourself. The very best way to invest in yourself is to incorporate others who you look up to, trust and respect, those people in your life who care about you, love you, and are willing to challenge you to be your best. Those who are honest with you even when you don't want to hear it. Those who love you even when your actions have them not liking you very much. Those who never give up on you even when you are giving up on yourself. Those who have taken the road less traveled, faced their own adversity, learned from it, and persevered. Those people in your life who I consider to be true heroes, a gift from the universe, and in its purest form, grace. For me, they are those people who have given to me without condition, often at their own expense, so that I could have a better life—my mentors.

Mentorship was not a new thing for me. I had been very fortunate to have what I believe to be some of the best people on the planet before the road to purpose. They helped me navigate careers, they were empathetic with the sometimes-unbearable sadness I was facing, and they put me back in the game when I simply wanted to quit. They helped me achieve things like success, status, career, and awards. They helped me realize my goals for fame and fortune and the work that produced both. So, mentorship was a big part of who I was, and like so many things along the road to purpose, it is essential to this day but has drastically changed in the way that it has impacted my life.

What changed was mentoring after the trip. The people who were part of my tribe approached me with questions versus answers. Hard questions, open-ended questions that forced me to explore ideas like purpose and values and other touchy-feely stuff. Questions that came without judgment that resulted in my finding the solutions that pushed me forward. What I would discover was that not just one but a team of mentors would help guide my way. As they had before, they would hold me accountable and push me to be better than I had ever been. They would care about me enough to not accept average, to pick me up when I stumbled, and to ensure that I didn't fall into despair.

So often, it isn't knowing what to do; it's doing it, and usually, that involves the fear of starting in the first place. If we are truly honest with ourselves, most of us often move on to the next shiny object, find excuses, or simply procrastinate and never reach our destination. Mentors help us focus and keep going. Today, my mentors are not just older people I know; they are also younger people, coworkers, mentees, and others who impact me every day. Others are people I have never met, community leaders and people in my field who challenge my thinking through their books, seminars, and events.

With that came something I was not comfortable with and had spent my entire life believing was a characteristic of the weak, the below-average, and those who I would often use to propel my selfish self ahead—that characteristic? Vulnerability. Yes, to be vulnerable in the eyes of others. To admit you have flaws, that you are scared and not sure of yourself. That you need help. Let me say that again: that you need help.

That is a tough thing to admit, and for me, well, I had attempted to do it alone. And what did I get? Depression, anxiety, and peering over the edge to a life no more. Keeping that fear inside and not trusting others took a toll on me. Being vulnerable by sharing a story for the first time lifted a massive weight off my shoulders that had been there for a couple of decades. A load that, once removed, has freed me to go after my best life.

My life today is full of courage instead of fear, curiosity instead of status quo, and compassion instead of narcissistic selfishness all because of that first step toward vulnerability. The mentors who gave me this gift did so by sharing their vulnerability with me and, in turn, making it okay for me to do the same. They are true heroes to me, some of the most courageous people I have ever known, and the single most significant impact on my life ever since. I will share their stories and the life-changing impact they made on me in the next section of the book, but first, let's take a look at those heroes from my past that are still with me today.

Standing on the Shoulders of Giants

The road to purpose had me thinking about all the great people I had in my life who had, often at tremendous personal sacrifice, been there for me in good and bad times. They encouraged me, they kicked me in the ass when I needed it, they cried with me and celebrated victories with me. They were always there, they always helped me find my way, and they never judged me. Some family, many friends and coworkers, and some with whom I had no relationship at all were there when I needed it.

People like my very first mentor, my maternal grandmother. She was one of the strongest women I knew yet could be vulnerable in her times of struggle and in turn made it okay for me to be vulnerable as well. She was the one person who was always there to listen—I mean listen and hear the message beyond the words. The person who understood me even when I didn't recognize myself. The person who, at my darkest hour when I didn't want to go on, showed up just in time to save my life. The person who ensured I had every experience yet held me responsible for working for it. She was the daily mass Catholic who believed in things like women's rights and gay rights and had no problem challenging a priest when she didn't agree with his position on a political topic of the day. She was an advocate of social justice and helping those less fortunate even when she didn't have a lot herself.

My grandmother was so much a part of the boy I was and, to this day, impacts the man I have become. Her words were with me along the road to purpose, helping reveal the part of myself that had been buried for so long. She was a ball of energy, never an excuse or blame, always forgiving others until her final days. It was her who I never had the chance to say goodbye to yet didn't need to because she is all around me, in me, and still guiding me to this day.

It seems so cliché, but by far, I got most of my learning from my parents. My mother, a clinical social worker, spent most of my teen years dealing with the hateful and obstinate behavior of me suffering silently from depression and hiding yet taking it out on everyone around, especially her. An expert in her field, she was fighting a mess at home that most likely ranked up there with her patients in the state-run youth reform school where she worked. I thank her for not giving up on me and for being tough when I tried to break her while knowing full well that she was unbreakable. For not accepting excuses and, at times, putting me back in the game when I didn't want to go. It was tough growing up, and sometimes it pushed me to the limit, but knowing what I know now, I would have never survived without my mother giving me no other choice but to do so.

And for my Dad, by far the best businessman I have ever met and my introduction to the family business. He taught me that you could build something from scratch with few resources and a big idea. He taught me to take care of the customer, to get involved and give back to my community, to protect my name and my credit, to set high expectations of myself, and that anything was possible if I was willing to work for it. He required that I get an education and work for someone else before I could return to the family business. I thank him for accepting me when I didn't make it back home to run the now third-generation businesses that he founded. For the foundation that led to an intrapreneurial approach to corporate life that eventually led to 30+ years of working for great American companies, companies that provided me with a couple of master's degrees, a wealth of experience, and a perspective on business that combined with cutting-edge tools that I now use in my own business coaching firm.

What he gave me was confidence and a sense of responsibility to use my talents in service to others. The courage to start my own company. The confidence that I, in turn, provide to my clients and those I mentor. The determination to know that inside of each of us is the capacity to achieve our greatest dreams. After the road to purpose, I did just that. Why I didn't take the opportunity to take over the family business, I got the "founder bug" late in life to start my own. I guess I was taking after him way more than I thought at the time.

As I look back on my time at home, I realized that one of the valuable lessons is the importance of seeking out experts, guides, and people who help you navigate the long stretches of the rough waters of life. People who have tried, failed, tried again, and found success. For me, the biggest secret in life is finding and reaching out to people who care enough to help you on your journey, to be honest with you even when you don't want to hear it, to love you, to provide precious time, the time they will never get back, to help you find your own way.

Put simply, life never happens alone, and these angels are the most cherished gift on earth. Mentors sometimes go unnoticed, and like purpose, I believe they are put in our lives for a reason at precisely the right time and place that helps you find and bring to life your meaning. They are the coaches, teachers, family members, friends, and strangers that give freely of themselves to help you grow. They can be older or younger, and often, the learning and love go both ways. They are guardian angels in every way. They are the people who make us great, they are the grace in our lives, they push us, they change our lives in every way. I would be nothing but a speck of dust floating aimlessly in the wind without them. They are the "master of the universe" in human form.

Mentors, coaches, and teachers do just that: They make sure we do what we say we will do. They help us craft a solution then walk beside us along the way to make sure that we bring that dream, that goal, to life. They are a proverbial stream of consciousness that provides our need at precisely the right time to thrive, grow, and excel. Find your "stream of life." Connect with mentors and angels, and put an accountability system in place to actually "get it done." I have found that allowing people to coast through life undermines an organization, destroys a person's self-esteem, and in turn, creates a system of dependence, blame, excuses, and entitlement that negatively impacts all involved.

On the other hand, having a trusted mentor to hold you accountable shows that "what we do matters." Accountability says that "who we are matters," and when we matter, self-confidence and the courage to push the limits for goal achievement seem a little closer. A culture of accountability with an influential mentor there to push you through will build the resilience you need to overcome the pain of transition, to know that you matter and that what you offer the world matters. The joy of mentorship applies to both young people joining the adult world as well as experienced people facing a career change, family change, or any other painful yet meaningful change in life.

So, how do you find a great mentor, or better yet, become a great mentor yourself? First off, to be a mentor is a gift you give your mentor; ironically, you bestow the gift of meaning and purpose upon them. By asking someone to share their knowledge, their wisdom, and their life experiences, you are honoring the person you are requesting the help from. You are giving them a gift in asking, the gift of meaning and purpose. When you ask someone to mentor you they share their lives with you, and you share yours with them: two people growing together, pure love in every way.

The road to purpose is all about two distinctly different generations who are facing similar pain and frustration of transition in their lives. One is figuring out what to do and the other figuring out what to do next. Both are wanting to impact the world positively, both looking for meaning and purpose. Mentoring is how the older generation can share wisdom with the young and the younger can help the older remain relevant. Wisdom and relevance—wow, what an opportunity for a beautiful life.

Give Back to Get Back

The road to purpose showed me many things, but one thing it brought to the forefront was the knowledge that my purpose was to help others. The thing I discovered was that I had been doing just that in my free time away from work. My volunteer work had initially been for financial reasons, to build a resume, to network with people in the new town I would later call home.

What I found was that the feeling of doing so would go way beyond merely being a way to meet people to help me get ahead. It would become the actual thing I did each day that brought joy to my life. What I found was that when I helped young people through mentoring roles, I learned something every day about them, about society and, most importantly, about myself—things that made me happier and a better person in problem-solving, all of which resulted in doing better at work and, in turn, being rewarded for it financially. By giving, I was getting back.

Courageous Leadership

At this point on the journey, it was time to fill that space up with talent and bring it to life by helping others. It was going to be difficult, but I was confident that I could pull together a team of mentors to help me get it done. Combining my talent aligned with a leadership role of some kind would be the answer. I had led teams before and enjoyed it. I had volunteered before with mentoring organizations like Big Brothers Big Sisters and SigEp and got a lot of fulfillment out of the relationships and progress experienced first-hand with the young people I mentored. So maybe I should look into something that brought those two things together.

So, what does it mean to be a mentor? To this point, we have talked about feeding yourself in several ways, including surrounding yourself with the right people, like mentors, coaches, and heroes.

What about you, who are you mentoring? One of the greatest things that I have learned about mentoring is that you get back way more than you give. Those are successful mentoring relationships, when the learning goes both ways. And as it often does, you learn more from teaching than being taught. To be a mentor takes knowledge, skills, experiences, patience, and a very, very big heart. It also takes courage and the ability to lead by example, the ability to be a true servant leader. Leadership is simple, inspiring others to act, to "want to" versus being directed to. To inspire action toward a common goal is the definition of leadership. So, ask yourself: Am I truly a leader in my organization? Do I help others realize their best life so that I can recognize my own? Am I willing to make the hard decisions when required? Do I listen to understand the needs of others before acting? Do others follow me because of the example I set, my character, or because of my age, rank, or position in life?

Together, mentorship and leadership become the true meaning of being a servant leader. I have found that combined, both resources define great leaders. Great leaders are a combination of who they are and what they do. They have a clear understanding of why they do what they do and consciously work on being better leaders every day. Great leaders are compassionate. They genuinely care about those they lead. The road to purpose made it perfectly clear that I would help organizations provide leadership development for their teams. I would help universities, young professionals, and student organizations prepare for their futures.

How about you? How might you use your talents to better the lives of someone else? Are you willing to get the training to fill the gaps that are relevant in today's world?

Three Key Signposts Along the Road to Purpose

1. Mentors comes in every form: family, teachers, coaches, and so many more.
2. Your best learning is from teaching others, having a mentor, and being a mentor.
3. Be a mentor, a servant leader, and you will find you learn as much as you teach.

SECTION IV

ASPIRE TO INSPIRE GREATNESS

*"What you leave behind is not what is
engraved in stone monuments,
but what is woven into the lives of others."*

—Pericles

Chapter 11

Building Balanced Men

*"You can be successful by yourself but
never significant without a team."*

—John Maxwell

My early adult life and the life I live today has come full circle. The road to purpose brought all those memories and all those people who had once meant so much to me back into my life after 30 years. Like many who became men in the '80s, I put my all into building a successful career. Success meant money and the trophies bought with cash. I recall a couple of sayings that went something like this: *The man with the most toys at the end of the game wins,* and *greed is good. Wow,* was that wrong. For me at the time, everything else had to take a second seat to my quest for career greatness. And I did just that. Relationships wasted time—no time for health, seeing the family on occasion. Fraternity brothers? Well, they just kind of faded away. Next thing you know, it's 30 years later, and I have achieved all my goals and continued to look for more, and I was empty. That pain was intense, and I was once again asking myself, *Is this all there is?*

Then, out of nowhere, the thought entered my mind that I needed to get back to being involved with the fraternity that I had left so long ago. You know, those thoughts you can't shake that come to you as if it were yesterday? My return to the fraternity was one of those thoughts for me.

The thought that I would volunteer after being away for so long was encouraged by the fact that the "every two-year conclave," a fraternity convention, was just down the road in Tennessee. I thought, *Wow, I'll sign up and drive down.* Well, that never happened. I had signed up all right, but less than an hour out of town, the voices in my head started talking: *You're irrelevant; what are you doing? You're going to embarrass yourself. You're going to walk into the room, and everyone is going to stare at you, reject you.* Well, that ended with me turning around and heading home, signing it all off to "it was never meant to be."

I would come to find that whatever put that thought in my head was not letting go that easy. A couple of weeks later, something even more bizarre happened. Leading up to what I thought was a trip to the conference, I had signed up for the organization's Facebook group. That day, a tribute video came on for a past grand president who had battled throat cancer and finally passed. He was younger than me and had changed the world in so many brothers and others, and the love through tribute interviews from those on the video was overwhelming.

I never knew the man, but a tear ran down my cheek, followed by a torrential downpour of sobbing. I wanted to be him. He represented everything that I had buried deep inside and wanted to set free. I bet I watched that video 20 times before I picked up the phone and offered to volunteer. My call was met by the then-district governors saying that no spots were open at the time but that they would put my name on the list and when an opportunity was available, they would give me a call. Three weeks later, a spot became open, and it turned out to be a top volunteer role in the very town where I lived. Coincidence, random? Or grace?

A Lifetime Commitment of Brotherhood

I would become Chapter Counselor just weeks before my world would come crashing down around me at work. Who would have guessed that a group of young men entering their final years of college would enter my life through a fraternity volunteer role that I had just been appointed? Who would have thought that as my career was ending, the life I was born to live would begin?

The young men I would mentor were full of hope yet, at the same time, dripping with anxiety about their transition from boyhood to manhood while also moving from college life to the work world. Like me, they were scared to death about the uncertainty of what would follow.

They were much younger than me, yet they were suffering from the same debilitating fear and anxiety that I was feeling. A number of them were also dealing with depression that came with the unimaginable pressure to compete in a global world. This was real and parallel to the need to fit in or be someone on social media and everything else that would come with their transition. Who would have thought that two distinctly different generations, suffering the same uncertainty, would come together to provide each other with meaning and purpose?

My life, I now know, was destined for this time over a decade ago. Looking back now, the very fact that my wife and I didn't have children made it possible to commit the time to this incredible group of young brothers. Had we had children, they would most likely have been their age, suffering from all the issues that modern-day society has heaped upon them. A group of young men, brothers, the sons I never had, amazing young people with incredible brains and even bigger hearts now filled that spot in my heart that was left empty so many years ago. Brothers who wanted to change the world, who were compassionate and talented yet empty inside. Brothers who needed me at that very moment that I needed them in my life. Another coincidence? No. More like grace.

This Fraternity Will Be Different

The fraternity purpose had been consistent since its founding that, "This fraternity would be different." The fraternity would provide an experience to young men like no other fraternity at the time or ever since. It was the first to move beyond privileged Ivy League universities to land grant and teacher colleges across the Midwest. It was the first to eliminate discrimination based on religion or race six full years before the equal rights amendment was passed. And later, it was the first to allow LGBTQ+ members. The first to end traditional pledging programs, giving all members equal rights and responsibilities from day one. The first to enact a nationally recognized Balanced Man Programming to deliver leadership skills in 90 percent of the time young men are out of the classroom. And recently, the first to eliminate alcohol from fraternity houses and address the evil of mental health in young men across the country. Yes, this fraternity has a tradition of being different.

For me, though, the young men I was working with were different in their own right, diverse and unique in every way. The fraternity celebrated that difference instead of trying to mold the men into something they were not. That celebration of diversity held together by a common set of values was the glue that bound them. Being achievers, every one of them, resulted in tops in academics, sports, philanthropy, leadership programming, and all the marks that measure a successful college fraternity.

In a time where toxic masculinity has infested college fraternities, these guys were embracing the power of vulnerability with each other and making it okay to be not okay, to address issues like sexual violence and raise awareness for the horrible evil of suicide plaguing their age group. To bounce back from a brother's suicide by doubling down on programming to make suicide awareness and prevention a top priority, from disdaining hazing to bringing in national speakers and committing to help end hazing nationwide in all areas of college life. I had not seen this in men before and am grateful for having the opportunity to learn to be vulnerable myself. To love them and not feel weird about it. To learn that vulnerability is actually courage at the highest level and to experience it in a way that forever changed my heart.

Vulnerability and Valor

The road to purpose took me on many journeys, but the one that I spent with some of the most incredible young people in Greece was life-changing. Out of the blue, I received an invite to be a mentor on a program called the Quest to Greece, a role usually held for longtime volunteers of the organization. This one-of-a-kind program utilizes the teachings of ancient philosophers to help young men learn more about themselves and their place in the world, to address issues facing them and then take that learning back to improve the lives of others.

I was fortunate to be chosen as one of six mentors for the group. Each mentor, successful in their own right, was selected for their specific talents, and all were committed to helping young people grow and reach their full potential. At the time, just leaving corporate life and starting all over with my own business, I was anything but successful and not sure why I was asked to join the group. That invite was followed by a conflict with a family wedding for a godson that I adored and the painful choice that I would have to make to go to Greece or attend his wedding. The choice I made and the speed bump that occurred I now know was a test from the master of the universe to see if I was committed to a life of meaning and purpose, even though I didn't realize it at the time. Coincidence?

The scholars included a group of high achievers, ages 19 to 23, who had committed their lives to excellence and serving others. Of the 500 who applied for this world-class leadership program, 16 were selected, each a leader on their campus and in their communities, including in academics, sports, government, and other student organizations. Other young men had started their own companies or had committed their lives to their country through military service and community service or represented exceptional talents in the performing arts, politics, education, business, engineering, and other endeavors to serve the greater good.

You may be thinking, "Just another study abroad program?" I did too, but that is where this group, this time, and this place became very different, a perfect storm of sorts on the road to purpose. Before leaving the country, the question was posed to the exceptional young scholars, "Why do you think you were chosen to participate in this program?" The answers from this select group of people still haunts me to this day. Not a single one had thought that they deserved to be in the room. The young men assembled saw themselves as average, as undeserving, as no different than their peers. They saw what they had achieved as nothing special and unworthy of the adventure they were about to experience. While they put on the face of success that lived up to their resume, it would later prove to be a mask that covered up a completely different story.

That night, the group boarded our plane and left for Greece. Within hours of meeting for the first time, this group from all parts of the country, diverse in belief, orientation, politics, race, religion, heritage, and background, were communicating as if they had known each other all their lives. Each with their ideas and opinions held engaged and respectful discourse, accepted each other, and celebrated their differences. By the time we arrived, they had begun to build the bonds of trust and welcomed the adventure that was about to take place, all with open hearts and minds.

QTG began each day with an early morning discussion on the teaching of an ancient philosopher, followed by a group discussion of the modern-day application of the learning. Later that day, the scholars would walk in the footsteps of that philosopher, visiting the sights and history and people of the time. The tours were informative but also mentally and physically challenging. The afternoon would usually end with socializing before dinner, a quick swim in the hotel pool, followed by a group discussion each evening, some lasting well into the wee hours of the morning.

It was in the group discussions where the real character of the men assembled revealed themselves. Each scholar was assigned a topic to facilitate dialogue with the rest of the group. The topics, deep in meaning, were designed to help each reflect on their own lives and share if they chose to. Subjects were selected for their impact on societal leadership, like purpose, virtue, sound mind and body, knowing thyself and facing fears, intervention and brotherly love, truth, and knowledge, to name a few.

It was during these discussions that things changed—we changed. It was the very place where we could be human and overcome our differences in age, title, and opinion, and our diversity in all its forms became one. The very place where being human and taking responsibility for ourselves and each other became clear. The very place where each who faced unimaginable and sometimes horrific backgrounds addressed their fears, accepted their flaws, realized their highest potential, and decided to use it to do great things in the world—the very point where our lives were changed forever.

The guys, often overcompensating for their flaws, entered believing that, as leaders, they were required to be strong and confident and sacrifice themselves for those they were leading. They never allowed themselves to be vulnerable in front of others, to be human or labeled as what they believed to be weak in any way.

The night events changed all that. Whether it be a safe place or interacting with other peer leaders, they let go, revealed the baggage that had been haunting them, and embraced the group for support. As they did, they began to reach their full potential. You see, these ambitious, successful, and motivated individuals did not come by their success by the luck of birth or by any particular blessing. They came by it through the decision to do so, to set goals, work hard, and do what it takes to achieve them. They faced their own self-limiting beliefs, real challenges of high anxiety, addiction, and depression brought on by unattainable expectations by society, often families, and mostly their self-criticism. They faced rejection from those they loved most or trusted institutions for their sexual orientation or losing their very identity due to a life-changing injury or overcoming the suicide of a parent or best friend killed by war. They faced it by suffering personal torment brought on by mistakes and past actions in direct contradiction to their values.

They had to forgive themselves for the shame and hopelessness from thoughts of suicide, drug addiction, and unimaginable things that they each had buried deep inside, covered up by the images they fought so hard to maintain.

And it wasn't just the scholars who allowed themselves to reveal their darkest secrets in the group. The mentors did too.

These were extremely successful men in their fields, measured in wealth and fame, and all the while, we were putting these men on pedestals while they were working on letting go of decades of grief held deep inside. Successful, everyone one of them, and empty inside. These men, now heroes to me, laid it all on the line to help each other and, in turn, helped themselves. The lives these men would lead after the quest in service to others has been nothing short of miraculous.

In all their pain, they had decided instead to bring joy to others through their energy and personality. To reinvent themselves and have faith in their abilities. To have the courage to live out their purpose and be their authentic selves no matter what others thought. To trust themselves and each other, to pursue and achieve their goals. To take responsibility for their actions, never making excuses or blaming others when they stumbled. To allow themselves to make mistakes, learn from them, and keep moving forward. To see failure as a learning opportunity to adjust and do it again and again, never giving up until they achieve their goal. Did I say these guys were 19 years old? Wow.

Dave Cooper, Seal Team 6, said, "being vulnerable together is the only way to be invulnerable. Real courage is seeing the truth and speaking the truth to each other." This group of exceptional young men did just that and, in so doing, blurred the lines between scholar and mentor.

Mentors soon followed, titans of industry, business owners and celebrities, all shared their experiences as tears flowed down our faces. We opened our hearts and forgave ourselves as well for things we had done in our pasts that had been burdening us for years. Like the scholars, we also learned to be vulnerable, and in doing so, we all grew closer and opened our hearts for what was next.

For me, that was letting go of the shame of giving in to depression, quitting and planning to end my life decades ago. For others, it was business deals that deeply violated personal values and took advantage of friendships for money, pain caused by coming out decades ago when society and parents had little tolerance for such courage, questions of fidelity and all kinds of actions that left deep pain and sorrow with families. Young brothers, in sharing their pain, helped not-so-young brothers share their own and, in so doing, we helped each other free ourselves from the shackles of life that had been buried deep in our subconscious and that had been holding us back all our lives.

The fraternity that I had let life get in the way of serving after graduation had come back into my life and in a big way at precisely the right time when I needed it most. That gift continues to give through the faculty roles I am honored to deliver leadership programming to and through young men who I learn from as a chapter counselor every time we are together. Recently, I had the honor of accepting a position on the National Board of Directors this past summer at the biannual conclave.

Yes, I had left Sigma Phi Epsilon, but it had never left me. For that, I am grateful. For that and the thousands of hours a year my incredible life allows me to volunteer, to share time, talent, and treasure, which is the single greatest gift of purpose a man could ask for. A gift that, given the way it was delivered back into my life at precisely the right time in the middle of a terrifying transition period, can only be grace.

Returning to the road to purpose post-trip:

As it often does, my overactive mind took me on a little trip through hell the last couple of months and left several fences needing mending along the way. It also produced learning and action that has me back and going stronger than ever. I'm now surer than ever that often one must make a trip through hell to realize heaven. That the struggle is always temporary, more like speed bumps, really. That real friends, brothers hold you accountable even when it's hard. They help you see what you can't see in yourself. They forgive, they never give up on you, and they help you learn, help you find meaning. In the end, they make you better and ready to spread your wings and soar even higher.

Three Key Signposts Along the Road to Purpose

1. Sometimes the universe puts you right in the middle of tragedy and pain not for the help you will provide but for the help you will receive.
2. Your responsibility for supporting those who come after you is a gift.
3. Vulnerability is the only accurate measure of a man.

Chapter 12

The Pebble On The Pond

*"We impact the world first through our clients,
then their families, employees, companies,
communities, region county, and world."*

—Steve Thompson

As it often does, my return home left me re-charged and ready to take on what was next. The noise of the past now gone and the discovery that my purpose had been with me all along, I prepared to head out to take on the world. That notion of retirement was also gone and quickly replaced with a vision of giving back, using my talents and life experiences to help others quickly fill the void. Happiness became the goal, and I was going to do it by helping others achieve their goals and make a living doing exactly that.

Opportunity to Change the World

Along the road to purpose, the idea of coaching came into my life in the form of a business opportunity. When I left on my journey, I had fully intended to retire or play a small role of some kind in a small brewery startup. Never in a million years did I think I would start a coaching and training company. My wife's words haunt me to this day: "You have been a coach all your life."

When I returned home, I followed up on one of those business opportunities, a coaching company that had been started by a business guru named Brian Tracy. I had reached out and began going through something called a discovery process where I researched the company, talked with other coaches, and eventually went to a meeting called a "discovery day" where the CEO and his team went over the program in great detail.

Everything about what I learned about the company was in perfect alignment with what I wanted to do. They shared similar values and offered the opportunity to help small businesses achieve their dreams. Too perfect. What must be wrong with it? Those voices were back and saying to me, *What are you doing trying to own a coaching company?* I had pretty much talked myself out of the opportunity and planned on heading home the next day.

After our meeting, the team met for dinner, and the funniest thing happened. The people around the table, who I had just met, felt like people I had known all my life. We shared a similar set of values, a desire to help people, and a lot of skills acquired over decades of corporate experience. I was back in the game.

On the walk back to the hotel, the CEO, Steve, caught up with me. I thought, oh no, here we go, my mouth had gotten me in trouble again. Before he could speak, I quickly apologized for the pointed questions I had asked at the meeting earlier that day.

He said, "No, that's why I wanted to talk to you. You asked the exact right questions; it was good for all the prospects in the room to hear. Do you want to grab a beer and talk more about it?" I said sure, and that night, over a beer and an NBA playoff game, it all changed when I got to know the man who would become my partner in the venture. In his caring way, he asked questions and spent a lot of time listening to my responses. He was coaching me, and I didn't even know it at the time. When I expressed that

I didn't see how the company would allow me to recapture my income from my corporate job, let alone grow to a million-dollar company, his response was, "Why not?"

A question that would make me think about it. Why not? Then I asked him what would keep me from building a million-dollar company that helps people. He quickly said the only thing that can stop you is you! Me? Yes, you! Get out of your own way, and make it what you want it to be.

That night led to my owning a business coaching and training company as well as becoming the Area Developer for the international brand in Kentucky. That meant that I would not only be helping business clients achieve their dreams but that I would also be creating the opportunity for business ownership for others in the same place with their careers that I had been. The result of that night has led to incredible growth over the past four years and unlimited numbers of people who have more substantial businesses or better lives because of the great work we did together. Steve was the first to ask the right questions, and when I turned the questions back on him, he would reassure me with thoughts like, "The only thing in your own way of success is you. Get out of your own way." I would take those words to heart and now teach them to others. I was soon helping people for a living and doing what I was probably always meant to do.

My Focal Point

Owning a business was a big step and a significant risk. Leaving a stable six-figure job with benefits at 50 to start all over again at zero was taking a leap of faith. It was a terrifying thing that would require tapping into courage as I had never had to before. The first few months of my new company were a challenge, with new clients, new processes, new time constraints, and those old voices back in my head. What I learned along the road to purpose was that sometimes the hardest step is the first one and that courage is what it takes to make it.

With that lesson and a healthy dose of compassion, I would put the needs of others ahead of my own commercial interests. If I could help others have a better life first and bring my purpose to life in my work, I knew the money would follow. And follow it did. I would base my company on compassion and define my life by the belief that we have a responsibility to each other. Each of us has a unique and God-given purpose of serving others. I would inspire those that I help and be inspired by them.

I was also reminded that capitalism and social responsibility could and must live in harmony with each other. That profit was not something to be embarrassed by but something that could be used to do good in the world. With great opportunity comes great responsibility to help others have a better life. Later, these lessons would become so clear that what I was born to do all along was to coach, mentor, and be a beacon of hope for others. The road to purpose had taught me that while this newfound understanding seemed fresh and new, it had been with me all my life and would later resurface itself in surprising ways that I can only define as grace.

Superstars and Life-Changers

What I didn't know was that when you are in the business of helping people, sometimes those very people want to join you on the journey. As the master of the universe so often does, he brings exactly the right people together to change the world. Two of those people I met as a mentor now work with me and mentor me in ways I never imagine. We work together along with my wife to bring our lessons to the vulnerable young men who inspired the entire movement and, in doing so, help them navigate the real challenges that we faced along the way.

Whether our paths cross in the night to bring pain, learning, and growth only for an instant or whether it goes on forever, only the Universe can answer. But what I know is that I am different, I think differently, love differently, care differently because of their presence in my life. I am humbled every day by the amazing grace this team has brought to the world since the road to purpose. Yes, this family business we built together will leave a legacy for many years.

One thing that the road to purpose brought to the forefront was the idea of opening myself up to new thinking. Realizing that with wisdom doesn't always come all the answers. It's really about people and meeting them on their own terms. It's about seeing the good in them even when it's hard to find. It's about being open to the next generation, their passion, ideas, wisdom, and their hearts. It's allowing them to grow and build their own lives in service to others. That is what living a life of meaning and purpose is all about, and I am grateful for the opportunity to see it happening right before my eyes.

Three Key Signposts Along the Road to Purpose

1. Put your purpose to work, and everything else falls in place.
2. The only thing in your own way is you. Get out of your own way, and get going.
3. The universe often brings back those you help to continue the legacy.

Firewalkers and Mountain Climbers

"Live life fully while you're here. Experience everything. Take care of yourself and your friends. Have fun, be crazy, be weird. Go out and screw up! You're going to anyway, so you might as well enjoy the process. Take the opportunity to learn from your mistakes. Don't try to be perfect; just be an excellent example of being human."

–Tony Robbins

As life so often does, a life of meaning and purpose often comes with clues along the way. We simply don't take the time to experience them until a major life transition smacks us in the face. One for me was a favorite poem given to me by a random friend in college decades ago that I did not really understand the meaning of until I finished the road to purpose. That poem is "Desiderata" by Max Ehrmann, which gave me a clue decades ago. I include it here with hopes that you too will find hints for a fulfilling purpose-filled life that are so eloquently included in his work.

"Desiderata"

Go placidly amid the noise and the haste, and remember what peace there may be in silence. As far as possible, without surrender, be on good terms with all persons.

Speak your truth quietly and clearly; and listen to others, even to the dull and the ignorant; they too have their story.

Avoid loud and aggressive persons; they are vexatious to the spirit. If you compare yourself with others, you may become vain or bitter, for always there will be greater and lesser persons than yourself.

Enjoy your achievements as well as your plans. Keep interested in your own career, however humble; it is a real possession in the changing fortunes of time.

Exercise caution in your business affairs, for the world is full of trickery. But let this not blind you to what virtue there is; many persons strive for high ideals, and everywhere life is full of heroism.

Be yourself. Especially do not feign affection. Neither be cynical about love; for in the face of all aridity and disenchantment, it is as perennial as the grass.

Take kindly the counsel of the years, gracefully surrendering the things of youth.

Nurture strength of spirit to shield you in sudden misfortune. But do not distress yourself with dark imaginings. Many fears are born of fatigue and loneliness.

Beyond a wholesome discipline, be gentle with yourself. You are a child of the universe no less than the trees and the stars; you have a right to be here.

And whether or not it is clear to you, no doubt the universe is unfolding as it should. Therefore be at peace with God, whatever you conceive Him to be. And whatever your labors and aspirations, in the noisy confusion of life, keep peace in your soul. With all its sham, drudgery and broken dreams, it is still a beautiful world. Be cheerful. Strive to be happy.

By Max Ehrmann © 1927 Original text

Awe and Wonder

Like many of you, I approached transition with fear, uncertainty, and anger. I was forced to live a life that I had not planned because of no fault of my own, and it sucked! I cannot wish the journey on anyone, but I can tell you this: I am grateful for it. Learning about myself, finding the courage to be me, and the newfound love for myself was life-changing for me, and I believe it can be for you too.

Whether you are moving from youth to adulthood, from a lifetime of successful work to jobless, you too can gain the grace gifted to you through the pain. When we gain some perspective, truly judge that perspective, and get to work on learning from it, you will find a life on the other side of struggle that is unimaginable. The grass is always greener on the other side if you choose for it to be. Since the road to purpose, my life has been nothing short of amazing, and yours can be too.

The past few years have been full of happiness, fulfillment, wealth, love, awe, and wonder. As this book approaches its final chapter, I see my life just beginning. It's an opportunity to share the grace I received, and it's a responsibility to help others see the possibility in themselves through my journey. To turn that pain into grace. To show through my own experience that deep understanding of myself, give myself the permission to be the man I always was, and to love and accept myself, for that was something that had been out of reach most all my life, and it was holding me back. Always moving forward at any cost meant pleasing people along the way, and that had become exhausting. The me who was continually grinding, burning candles at both ends, leaving people behind along the way, turned out to be all for naught.

Before long, the trip was long gone, and the new me, the real me, was ready for the next chapter in my life. The anger was gone, the despair and limiting beliefs had been left alongside the road somewhere, and the new life that I was about to embark upon was both scary as hell and exciting at the same time. What I didn't know was the profound impact it would have on me, the rate of change that would excite me, or the people and situations that would seemingly come into my life without reason—people who would change my life in ways I could have never dreamed.

What happened next leaves me full of awe and wonder. It leaves me grateful for the opportunities provided to me by the master of the universe and a little hard work, for the results and the achievement that have come to me while focusing on helping others be their best. All of this is there for you to realize as well on the other side of your own transition.

Awe and wonder. I am grateful every day for that day almost five years ago when my old company allowed me to go on the incredible journey, a journey of self-discovery. Without that day,

I would have stayed comfortable in my cushy, high-profile marketing job. I would have never taken a two-month random road trip, or even a not-random one. I would have never revisited the people who mattered in my life, long forgotten by the demand of corporate life, or the excuse of one, anyway. I would have never seen the beautiful country we call home, especially the "flyover states" we so often made fun of. And I would have never emptied all the stress, anger, noise, and poison in my brain that inevitably would have shortened my time on earth. The incredible life I have today would never have happened had it not been for a short-sighted decision to sell a brand and the heartless impact that had on so many people.

If it had not been for that day, I would not own my thriving and successful company, a company that helps people every day have a better life. If it weren't for that day, I would have never met the people who I have had a chance to meet and received the profound impact that they have had on my life. If it weren't for that day so many years ago, I would not have the opportunity to work with my wife and a team of incredible people who spend every day trying to make life better for others. If that day had not happened, I would not have the freedom to mentor a full day a week, changing the lives of young people while they change mine in so many ways. The master of the universe is working in so many ways in our lives. Those who live the purpose they were born with are serving the very universe in which we live. If not for that day, my eyes would have never been opened to the humble pain that has inspired more growth in my heart than I have accumulated over a lifetime.

Awe and wonder. The past four years have been unimaginable, humbling, and scary. The experience since the road to purpose opened my mind and my heart to all that has followed. That, with the grace of God, has become the most incredible thing in my life ever since. This is a book that in and of itself would never have happened had it not been for the series of random and coincidental events that occurred in my life. You now have the same opportunity to turn your transition into an amazing life and experience the same awe and wonder in your own journey.

So, what have been the personal results from living a life of purpose since the journey? The life-changing events include significant changes in my wellness, relationships, work, wealth, wisdom, and world impact. Grace is what has been the result ever since. Let me share just a few things that have come from that most horrible of days not that long ago in hopes that you will too see that those challenges, fears, and limiting beliefs are holding you back. The golden handcuffs have rusted, and your true destiny, the best days of your life, lie ahead. You too will find unimaginable happiness, wealth, love, and personal growth like never before if you merely breathe and take that first step. During this time, I created a simple tool to track my progress, my life plan. I call it the "Web of Life" and use it to track my progress in six essential areas: wellness, we relationships, work, wealth, wisdom, and world impact.

First, wellness. For me, this means a sound mind, body, and spirit. In the years that followed the road to purpose, I have lost 70 pounds and ten inches around the waist, something I haven't realized since my days in college. I have more energy and can keep up the rapid pace of my life today. I am now setting goals to live to 110 years old. My brain is under control through a regular morning routine that includes 45 minutes of exercise five days a week. I am spiritually at peace, meditating daily. I even had the courage to walk on a bed of hot coals, 2,000 degrees, which, believe me, takes a lot of mindfulness. I'm in the best shape of my life, mind, body, and spirit.

Next up, we relationships. What do I mean by "we relationships"? Well, exactly how it sounds: the times when we focus on we versus me. I believe that it is in human relationships where fulfillment occurs. We are not in this alone, and alone usually turns out to be a life of misery. My wife and I have just celebrated our 26th wedding anniversary, and our circle of friends, as diverse as the world itself, has quadrupled over the last few years. I get to work with some of the most incredible people who have become like family to me. The trip also reintroduced me to family and time to spend with them in their world, a world I had lost track of over the years. I got to spend some time with my family, nephews, aunts, and uncles whose lives are all moving as fast as my own. And my chosen family, the men in my fraternity. The group has now crossed well over 1,000 young men who share their life and I mine with them every year.

Third, work. I wake every day with a sense of purpose and help others achieve their dreams, reach their goals, and overcome their challenges, just as I did throughout this process. My income over the past four years has exceeded what I worked for for 30 years. We are expanding and making the opportunity of business ownership available to others. My network has grown to 5,000+, and I have a personal relationship with my clients (friends, really) that I could only have dreamed of.

Fourth, wealth. Depending on how you define it, it has expanded, my debt is gone, and my non-financial wealth has grown exponentially. My investments have nearly doubled in size, and we are now able to share that wealth with others who need it. The road to purpose has shown me that you really can have your cake and eat it too.

Fifth, wisdom. Wow, this one has grown in significant ways. Merely going through the life lessons of the last few years has changed me completely. The experience alone is worth millions. The pain, overcoming the anxiety, and turning it into the most beautiful life has improved my self-confidence and self-esteem in ways that I never thought possible. I have also become a prolific reader of books, averaging 50+ a year in my field, something equivalent to an applied master's degree every two years. I also use that knowledge in workshops, talks, and seminars to bring it to life and share it with others.

Finally, world impact. Controlling my time, my money, and my life has allowed me to refocus my priorities in such a way that helps others. We are using money to establish scholarships for young people who need the opportunity to find their purpose and bring it to life through leadership programming. We are providing much-needed resources to help young people overcome mental health roadblocks and provide support and skill development for first-generation students, all to help build confidence and self-esteem in a way that promotes their authentic selves and gives them the tools to impact the world in a positive way.

Final Thoughts on the Road to Purpose

The past four years since the road to purpose have been nothing short of grace. I found that the story and the life I have experienced was there for all of us to take advantage of, even when we may not see past the pain. I know now that growth, real human growth, can only come through transition, and the transition is often scary and painful and, more times than not, gets worse before it gets better. I also know that both young and not-so-young have a real gift to help each other through this transition and, in so doing, can both realize a life that at the time they never thought possible.

Who would have thought a random series of events could result in the most incredible life ever? It did for me, and it will work for you too. A journey that started in anger, blame, and negative thinking would turn out so wonderful. It was a trip where it took time to empty the anger, survive the empty feeling that was left, then fill it all up with purpose before taking on the world.

I invite you along to take your road to purpose so that you will know that you are here for a reason. The world is moving fast, and if we don't take the time to clear our minds of the noise, we will wake up one day, and it will be long gone. Sometimes, it takes pain to see what the universe has planned for us. While we can push through and move forward, if we are not in line with our purpose, we will move forward, but it will be painful. The people, the situations, and the pain are all for a reason: to make us better. To bring us closer to our maker and to do it all in service to others.

Review Inquiry

Hey, it's Greg here.

I hope you've enjoyed the book, finding it both useful and fun. I have a favor to ask you.

Would you consider giving it a rating wherever you bought the book? Online book stores are more likely to promote a book when they feel good about its content, and reader reviews are a great barometer for a book's quality.

So please go to the website of wherever you bought the book, search for my name and the book title, and leave a review. If able, perhaps consider adding a picture of you holding the book. That increases the likelihood your review will be accepted!

Many thanks in advance,

Greg A. Pestinger

Will You Share the Love?

Get this book for a friend, associate, or family member!

If you have found this book valuable and know others who would find it useful, consider buying them a copy as a gift. Special bulk discounts are available if you would like your whole team or organization to benefit from reading this. Just contact https://p3peakperformance.com/contact/ or call 502.409.9453.

Would You Like Greg Pestinger to Speak to Your Organization?

BOOK GREG NOW!

Greg accepts a limited number of speaking/coaching/training/consulting engagements each year. To learn how you can bring his message to your organization, call 502.409.9453 or email https://p3peakperformance.com/contact/.

Forthcoming Book

The Road to Purpose shows us that we can overcome seemingly insurmountable mountains through the way we approach our lives. That when we push past our limiting beliefs, when we truly get to know ourselves, have the courage to be ourselves, and find the strength to love who we are, anything is possible.

If *The Road to Purpose* was all about lining up behind a life of meaning and purpose, my next book, *Firewalkers and Mountain Climbers*, gives us the "how" to go about making real change in our life. How do we realize the life we have alway been looking for by finding balance then taking massive intentional action? *Firewalkers and Mountain Climbers* will provide you the road map to achieving success in all areas of your life, including wellness, relationships, work, wealth, wisdom, and world impact. Take action now and realize your own life of meaning and purpose.

About the Author

Greg Pestinger is a performance coach, trainer, mentor, author, and speaker who works with high-performing individuals and business leaders to identify their authentic selves, build their unique brands, identify their passions, and lead lives of meaning and purpose. In short, he utilizes simple tools and strategies to help them realize their full potential quicker than they could on their own. He believes that at the heart of success is the ability to capitalize on our authentic self in service to others.

For the past 30 years, Greg has achieved unprecedented revenue, profit, and market share growth in senior executive roles for some of America's largest and most respected brand companies, including Pepsi, General Electric, Anheuser-Busch InBev, and Brown Forman. He holds numerous certifications and has been recognized for brand-changing advertising as a global brand strategist. He has taught teams to dream big, believe in themselves, and never give up. These teams have realized their full potential and, in turn, lived more productive and more fulfilling lives. Today, Greg is a certified business performance coach, trainer, author, and speaker. He is an authority on Human Potential and Courageous Leadership and the recipient of the prestigious Campbell Fraser Award for Coaching Excellence.

Greg holds a BS in Marketing, an MA degree in Human Resource Development, and an MBA in Organizational Leadership. He volunteers his time helping young people identify their purpose with mentoring organizations including Big Brothers Big Sisters, Sigma Phi Epsilon Education Foundation, and the University of Louisville. Greg and his wife Donna live in Louisville, Kentucky, where they own and operate Pestinger Peak Performance Inc., Thomas Alan Properties, and FocalPoint Coaching and Training Excellence of Kentucky.

Greg believes that life has meaning and purpose. He believes that each of us has an unlimited capacity to achieve our greatest dreams and realize our full potential. He has committed his life to helping people by applying proven strategies and tools to help them realize their full potential so that they can positively impact the world.

Greg can be reached at:
www.p3peakperformance.com